The Art of
Patience

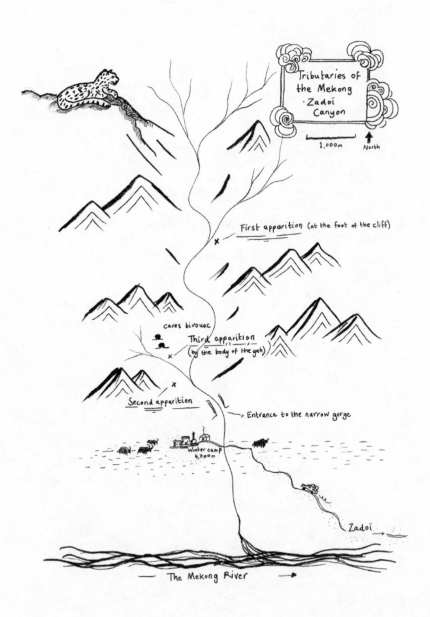

Tributaries of
the Mekong
·Zadoï
Canyon

1,000m

North

First apparition (at the foot of the cliff)

caves bivouac

Third apparition
(by the body of the yak)

Second apparition

Entrance to the narrow gorge

Winter camp
4,100m

Zadoï

— The Mekong River →

The Art of
Patience

*Seeking the
Snow Leopard in Tibet*

SYLVAIN TESSON

Translated from the French by Frank Wynne

PENGUIN PRESS | *New York* | 2021

PENGUIN PRESS

An imprint of Penguin Random House LLC

penguinrandomhouse.com

LIBRARY OF CONGRESS CATALOGING-IN-PUBLICATION DATA

Names: Tesson, Sylvain, 1972– author. | Wynne, Frank, translator.
Title: The art of patience: seeking the snow leopard in Tibet /
Sylvain Tesson; translated from the French by Frank Wynne.
Other titles: Panthère des neiges. English
Description: New York: Penguin Press, 2021. |
Includes bibliographical references.
Identifiers: LCCN 2020052516 (print) | LCCN 2020052517 (ebook) |
ISBN 9780593296288 (hardcover) | ISBN 9780593296295 (ebook)
Subjects: LCSH: Tibet Autonomous Region (China)—Description and travel. |
Tesson, Sylvain, 1972– —Travel—Tibet Autonomous Region (China) |
Snow leopard—Tibet Autonomous Region (China)
Classification: LCC DS786 .T45413 2021 (print) |
LCC DS786 (ebook) | DDC 915.1/504612—dc23
LC record available at https://lccn.loc.gov/2020052516
LC ebook record available at https://lccn.loc.gov/2020052517

Printed in the United States of America
1st Printing

Designed by Cassandra Garruzzo

To the mother of a lion cub

The females of all animals are less violent in their passions than the males, except the female bear and the leopard, for the female of these appears more courageous than the male.

ARISTOTLE
The History of Animals, IX

CONTENTS

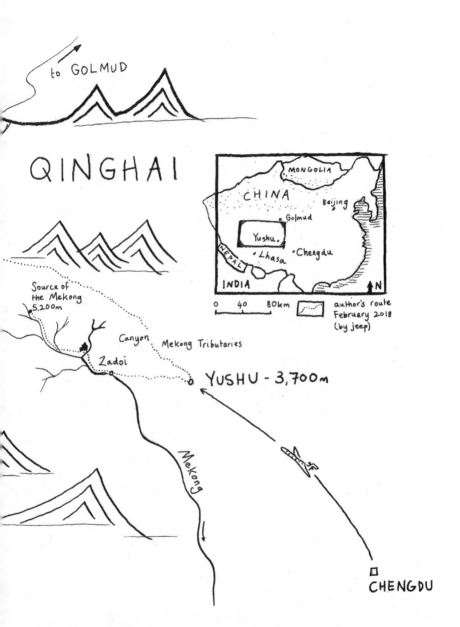

to GOLMUD

QINGHAI

MONGOLIA

CHINA   Beijing

Golmud

Yushu.

NEPAL   • Lhasa   • Chengdu

INDIA

0   40   80km   author's route
                     February 2018
                     (by jeep)

Source of
the Mekong
5,200m

Canyon   Mekong Tributaries

Zadoï

YUSHU - 3,700m

Mekong

CHENGDU

PREFACE

I had met him one Easter day, at a screening of his film about the Abyssinian wolf. He had spoken to me about the elusiveness of animals and of the supreme virtue: patience. He had told me about his life as a wildlife photographer, and explained the technique of lying in wait. It was a delicate and rarefied art that involved hiding in the wild and waiting for an animal that could not be guaranteed to appear. There was a strong chance of coming away empty-handed. This acceptance of uncertainty seemed to me to be very noble—and by the same token anti-modern.

Could I, who loved to run like the wind over lowlands and highlands, manage to spend hours, silent and utterly still?

Lying among the nettles, I obeyed Munier's precepts: not

a movement, not a sound. I could breathe; this was the only vulgar reflex permitted. In cities, I had grown accustomed to prattling about anything and everything. The most difficult thing was saying nothing. Cigars were prohibited. "We'll smoke later, down by the river," Munier had said, "it will be night and fog!" The prospect of lighting a Havana on the banks of the Moselle made it easier to endure the position of prostrate watcher.

Life was exploding. The birds in the trees streaked the night sky, they did not shatter the magic of the place, did not disturb the order of things, they belonged to this world. This was beauty. A hundred meters away, the river flowed. Swarms of dragonflies hovered over the surface, predatory. On the western bank, a hobby falcon was diving. Its flight was hieratic, precise, deadly—a Stuka.

This was not the time to allow myself to be distracted: two adult badgers were emerging from the sett.

Until it grew dark, all was a mixture of grace, of drollery, of authority. Would the badgers give a signal? Four heads appeared, and the shadows darted from the tunnels. The twilight games had begun. We were posted ten meters away, and the animals were oblivious to our presence. The badger cubs tussled, scrabbled up the embankment, rolled into the ditch, nipped at each other's necks and got a clout from an adult, determined to restore a semblance of order to the night circus. The black pelts daubed with three stripes of ivory would disappear into the undergrowth only to reappear further on. The animals were preparing to forage in the fields and on the riverbanks. They were warming up for the night ahead.

From time to time, one of the badgers would wander close to our hide, snuffling the ground with its long snout, then turning to face us. The dark bands set with coal-black eyes sketched out melancholy smears. They were still on the move; we could make out the powerful plantigrade paws turned inward. In the French clay, their claws left small bear-like tracks that a certain lumbering race of humans, in its wisdom, identified as the tracks of "vermin."

It was the first time I had ever been so still, hoping for an encounter. I scarcely recognized myself. Until now, from the Yakutia to Seine-et-Oise, I had run, adhering to three principles:

- The unexpected does not pay house calls, it must be sought out everywhere.
- Movement enhances inspiration.
- Boredom runs less swiftly than a man in a hurry.

In short, I convinced myself that there was a link between distance and the importance of an event. I thought of stillness as a dress rehearsal for death. In deference to my mother, resting in the family tomb on the banks of the Seine, I roved about frenetically—the mountains on Saturday, the seaside on Sunday—without paying attention to what was going on around me. How do journeys spanning thousands of kilometers lead one day to lying in the tall grass with your chin propped on the edge of a ditch?

Next to me, Vincent Munier was taking photographs of the badgers. The mass of muscle beneath his camouflage clothes blended into the vegetation, but his profile was still visible in the half-light. His face, all sharp edges and long ridges, seemed to be sculpted for issuing orders; he had a nose that Asians mocked, a carved chin and soft eyes. A gentle giant.

He had talked to me about his childhood, his father taking him to a hide beneath a spruce tree to witness the flight of the king—the capercaillie; the father teaching the son the promise of silence; the son discovering the rewards of nights spent lying on the frozen ground; the father explaining that the appearance of an animal is the greatest gift life can give to those who love it; the son setting up his own hides, discovering the secrets of the world unaided, learning to frame a nighthawk taking wing; the father discovering the son's artistic photographs. Munier, lying next to me, had been born in the mists of the Vosges. He had become the greatest wildlife photographer of his time. His peerless photographs of wolves, bears and cranes were sold in New York galleries.

"Tesson, I'm taking you to the forest to see badgers," he had said to me, and I had accepted, because no one refuses an invitation from an artist in his studio. He did not know that

Tesson meant "badger" in Old French. The word is still common in the vernacular of western France and Picardy. It originated as a deformation of the Greek *taxis*, from which we get the words "taxonomy," the science of classifying animals, and "taxidermy," the art of stuffing animals (since man likes to skin the things he has just named). On the topographical maps of France, there are *tessonières*, the name given to the bucolic sites of mass culls. For, in the countryside, the badger was despised and ruthlessly destroyed. It was accused of digging up the soil, of damaging hedges. It was smoked out, it was killed. Did the badger deserve the relentless fury of men? It was a secretive animal, creature of night and solitude. It favored an inconspicuous life, ruled over the shadows, did not suffer visitors. It knew tranquility was something to be defended. It left its sett at night and returned at dawn. How could man tolerate the existence of a totem to discretion, making a virtue of distance and an honor of silence? Zoologists described the badger as "monogamous and sedentary." If etymology connected me to the animal, I did not conform to its nature.

NIGHT FELL, THE ANIMALS disappeared into the undergrowth, there was a general rustling. Munier must have noticed my joy. I considered these few hours as one of the best nights of my life. I had just encountered a clan of living creatures that was utterly sovereign. They did not struggle to escape their condition. We headed back to the road via the riverbank. In my pocket, the cigars were crushed.

"There's an animal in Tibet that I've been tracking for six years," said Munier. "It lives up in the high plateaus. You can spend a long time in a hide just to catch a glimpse of one. I'm going back this winter; come with me."

"What is it?"

"The snow leopard," he said.

"I thought it had disappeared," I said.

"That's what it wants you to think."

PART ONE

The Approach

The Goal

L ike skiing instructors in the Tyrol, snow leopards
make love amid silvery white landscapes. In February, they go into rut. Swathed in furs, they live amid
the ice. The males fight, the females offer themselves, couples
call to each other. Munier had warned me: if we were to have
a chance of spotting a snow leopard, we would have to track
it in the dead of winter, at an altitude of between 4,000 and
5,000 meters. I would try to counterbalance the discomforts
of winter with the joy of an apparition. It was a technique
Saint Bernadette had adopted in the grotto at Lourdes. While
the little shepherdess doubtless suffered from cold knees, the
sight of a Virgin ringed with a halo was worth it.

"Leopard": the very word chimed like precious stones.

There was no guarantee that we would encounter one. Hunting from a hide is a wager: you set out in search of an animal; you court failure. Some people are untroubled by this; they enjoy the anticipation. Sadly, I am not among them. I was determined to see the animal even if, out of politeness, I did not confess my impatience to Munier.

Snow leopards were widely targeted by poachers. This was another reason for making the journey. We would be visiting the bedside of a wounded creature.

Munier had shown me the photographs he had taken on previous expeditions. The beast combined power and grace. Its fur threw off sparks of glittering reflections, its paws were wide as saucers, it used its oversized tail as a balancing pole. It was adapted to living in inhospitable terrain and to scaling cliffs. It was the spirit of the mountain come to earth, an ancient creature forced into exile by the murderous rage of humans.

I associated the animal with a person: a woman who would never again travel anywhere with me. She was a child of the forests, queen of wild waters, friend to animals. I had loved her; I had lost her. In an ineffectual and infantile view, I associated her memory with an inaccessible animal. It is a prosaic syndrome: you miss a person, the world takes on her shape. If I encountered the animal, I would one day tell her that it was she I had chanced upon, on a winter's day on a snow-white plateau. It was magical thinking. I was afraid of seeming ridiculous. At the time, I did not say a word to my friends. But I thought about it constantly.

It was early February. To lighten our load, I made the mistake of wearing all my mountaineering gear. In a Paris suburb, I boarded a train for the airport wearing my Arctic jacket and my Chinese "long march" army boots. In a carriage filled with handsome Fulani knights of sorrowful countenance, and a Moldovan who was massacring Brahms on an accordion, I was the one people stared at, because my clothes were out of place. Exoticism had shifted.

We took off. Definition of progress (and thus of sadness): taking ten hours to cover a distance it took Marco Polo four years to cross. Unfailingly polite, Munier made the introductions while we were in the air. I greeted the two friends with whom I was about to spend a month: Munier's fiancée, Marie, a woman with a lithe body, a wildlife filmmaker obsessed with the wild and with extreme sports, and Léo, who had hypermetropic eyes, tousled hair and a philosophical mindset, and hence was taciturn. Marie had made a film about wolves, and another about the lynx, animals living on borrowed time. She was about to shoot a film about her twin loves: snow leopards and Munier. Two years earlier, Léo had interrupted his philosophical thesis to work as Munier's assistant. In Tibet, Munier needed aides-de-camp to set up the hides, to regulate his cameras, and as company in the long nights. Being unable to carry heavy loads due to a weak spine—I had broken my back in a fall from the roof of a friend's house in 2014, and my recovery had been long and grueling—and having not the slightest competence in matters of photography, or of tracking animals, I did not know what my role would be. It was my responsibility not to hold the others up and not to sneeze if the snow leopard appeared. I was being offered Tibet on a plate. I was off to find an insubstantial animal in the company of an accomplished artist, a human she-wolf with eyes of lapis lazuli and a brooding philosopher.

"We're the 'Gang of Four'!" I said, as the plane touched down in China.

At least I could supply the jokes.

The Center

We had landed at the easternmost point of Tibet, in the administrative province of Qinghai. The gray terraces of the city of Yushu, perched at an altitude of 3,700 meters, had been completely razed by an earthquake in 2010.

In less than a decade, fueled by colossal Chinese energy, the rubble had been banked up and the town completely rebuilt. Now, streetlamps in serried rows illuminated a perfectly smooth concrete grid of buildings. Cars moved slowly and silently over the streets of this checkerboard. The barracks-city foreshadowed its future as a permanent globalized building site.

It took three days to cross eastern Tibet by car. We were

headed south of the Kunlun Mountains, to the plateau of Changtang, where Munier knew steppes that abounded with wild animals.

"We'll take the main Golmud to Lhasa route," he had told me on the plane. "We're heading for the village of Budongquan, next to the railway."

"And from there?"

"We'll head west toward the foothills of the Kunlun Mountains, to the 'valley of the yaks.'"

"Is that what it's actually called?"

"It's what I call it."

I was scribbling in my black notebooks. Munier had made me promise that, if I wrote a book, I would not use real place names. These places had their secrets. If we were to reveal them, hunters would come and gut them. We adopted the habit of referring to places according to a poetic geography, one that was personal and sufficiently inventive to cover our tracks, yet vibrant enough to be precise: the valley of the wolves, the lake of the Tao, the cave of the mountain sheep. Henceforth, in my mind, Tibet would be a hand-drawn map of memories, less precise than those found in an atlas, appealing more to dreams, and preserving the sanctuaries of animals.

We drove northwest, through the stepped granite of the plateaus. At an altitude of 5,000 meters, gorge was followed by gorge, barren hill by mountain herd. Winter created rare plaques of ice on flat terrain where the wind raged furiously. The firn did little to smooth the outcrops.

Feral eyes were doubtless watching from the ridges, but in a car there was nothing to see except my reflection in the window. I did not see so much as a wolf. The wind whipped up a gale.

The air had a metallic tang, its harshness uninviting; it did not stir the urge to ramble or to return.

The Chinese government had carried out its project of subjugating Tibet. Beijing was no longer interested in persecuting monks. To control a territory, there exists a more effective approach than coercion: humanitarian development and infrastructure. When central government provides creature comforts, revolution gutters out. If there is a communal uprising, the authorities indignantly bluster: "What do you mean an uprising? And here we are building schools!" A century earlier, Lenin had trialed this method with his "electrification of the whole land." Beijing had adopted the strategy as early as the 1980s. The logorrhea of Revolution had given way to logistics. The goal was simple: control vested in the center.

The road wound its way over rivers spanned by brand-new bridges. The peaks bristled with mobile phone masts.

Centralized control meant endless infrastructure projects. A railway line would cleave old Tibet from north to south. Lhasa, a city closed to foreigners until the middle of the twentieth century, was now a mere forty hours by train from Beijing. The portrait of the Chinese President Xi Jinping stared down from billboards: "Dear comrades," the slogans implied, "I'm bringing you progress, so shut your mouths!" Jack London neatly summed up the idea in 1903: "when one man feeds another he is that man's master."

Colonial villages flashed past, their concrete cubes affording shelter to Chinese men in khaki and Tibetan men whose blue overalls confirmed that modernization is the pauperization of the past.

In the meantime, the gods had retreated and the beasts with them. How could we hope to see a lynx in these valleys bristling with pneumatic drills?

The Circle

We were approaching the railway line; I was dozing in the livid air. The skin of Tibet was red raw. We were moving through a topography of granite planes and patches of soil. Outside, a sanatorium sun occasionally pushed temperatures above −20°C. Having little taste for barracks, we made no stops in the Chinese pioneer villages, opting instead for monasteries. In the courtyard of a Buddhist temple on the outskirts of Yushu, we witnessed the great confluence of pilgrims before shrines wreathed in the incense smoke. There were piles of Mani stones carved with Buddhist mantras: *Om mani padme hum*—"Praise to the Jewel in the Lotus."

Tibetans moved around the piles, spinning prayer wheels

with a flick of their wrist. A little girl offered her prayer beads, which I would spend the next month using as a rosary. A yak draped in a military jacket was chewing cardboard, the only living creature standing still. In order to acquire merits in the cycle of reincarnation, arthritic pilgrims pitted with scrofula crawled through the dust, their hands protected by wooden pads. They smelled of death and urine. The faithful moved in circles, waiting for this life to pass. From time to time, the circle was broken by horsemen from the high plateaus, who looked like Kurt Cobain—robes trimmed with fur, Ray-Bans and cowboy hats—knights of the great morbid merry-go-round. Like all glorious nomadic peoples, the Khampa love blood, gold, jewels and weaponry. These men had no rifles and no daggers. Long before the turn of the millennium, Beijing had forbidden civilians from carrying weapons. The civil disarmament had been good for wild animals: fewer people were shooting leopards. But psychologically, the effects had been disastrous, since a musketeer without a sword is an emperor without clothes.

"These circles make my head spin. They're like vultures wheeling above a carcass," I said.

"Sun and death," said Léo, "decay and life, blood in the snow: the world is a mill."

When you travel, always take a philosopher with you.

The Yak

The great body of Tibet was prostrate, ailing in the rarefied air. On the third day, we came to the railway line at an altitude of 4,000 meters. The tracks cut a gash through the steppe, starting in the north, running parallel to the tarred road. I had cycled the road to Lhasa fifteen years earlier, when work on the railway line had just begun. Since then, Tibetan laborers had died of exhaustion and yaks had learned to contemplate the passing trains. I remembered my struggle to cover every kilometer in these landscapes too vast for a bicycle. An effort was never rewarded by a nap in a mountain pasture.

A hundred kilometers to the north, having passed the village of Budongquan, we drove through the valley of the yaks promised by Munier. The road stretched away toward the sunset, along a frozen river bordered by banks of sand like pale silk.

To the north, the foothills of the Kunlun Mountains formed a frieze. At night, the peaks took on a reddish hue, silhouetted against the sky. By day, the glaciers melded into one. To the south, Changtang shimmered on the horizon, unexplored.

At 4,200 meters, the road passed a cob-wall cabin. Tranquility and light: a perfect real-estate bargain. We settled into our billet for our next few days, on narrow cots with wooden slates, the promise of swift nights. The openings cut into the walls afforded the sort of view of a line of peaks worn down by erosion that is the desolation of landscapes. Two kilometers to the south of our shelter, an oxidized granite dome rose to 5,000 meters: tomorrow, these peaks would serve as observation posts, but tonight they afforded an imposing overlook. To the north, a river meandered through a glacial trough five kilometers wide. This was one of the rivers of Tibet that never see the sea, since they disappear into the sands of Changtang. Here, even the elements accord with the Buddhist doctrine of extinction.

For ten days, we spent every morning scouring the surrounding area, striding across the glacis (Munier's loping gait). When we woke, we would climb 400 meters to the granite ridge above the shack. We would arrive there about an hour before daybreak. The air smelled of cold stone. It was −25°C: a temperature in which nothing was possible, neither movement, nor words, nor melancholy. We merely waited for day, filled with a numb hope. At dawn, a yellow blade cut through the night and, two hours later, the sun scattered its crumbs of light over the expanses of rock studded with tufts of grass. The world was frozen eternity. In such a cold, it seemed impossible that the landscape could crumble any further. But suddenly, the vast plain, revealed in the dawn light that I had believed deserted, became speckled with dark smudges: animals.

Out of superstition, I never mentioned the snow leopard; it appeared when the gods—the polite name for chance—decided that the moment was propitious. On this particular morning, Munier had other concerns. He wanted to get closer to the wild yaks that we had only seen as distant herds. He worshipped these beasts, he spoke of them in low murmurations.

"They are called *drong*, they are the reason I come back here."

In the bull, he saw the soul of the world, the symbol of fertility. I told him that the ancient Greeks slaughtered them and offered their blood to spirits of the underworld, the smoke to gods and the finest cuts to princes. Bulls offered a means of intercession; a sacrifice was an invocation. But Munier was more interested in the golden age before high priests.

"Yaks come from the dawn of time: they are the totems of life in the wild, you can see them drawn on Paleolithic walls, they have never changed, it's as though they've emerged, snuffling and snorting, from a cave painting."

The yaks punctuated the slopes with their great wads of black wool. Munier gazed at them with his pale, sorrowful eyes. As in a waking dream, he seemed to be counting the last lords making a farewell procession across the ridge.

These tattered pack animals with their oversized horns had been slaughtered by the Chinese colonists through the twentieth century, and the last surviving traces of the herds were to be found on the borders of Changtang and the Kunlun foothills. Since the awakening of the economic powerhouse in China, governmental agencies had been practicing intensive breeding. There were a billion and a half citizens to be fed, and the uniformity of world standards meant they could not be deprived of red meat. Veterinary agencies had crossed the wild yak with domestic breeds to create the *datong*, a hybrid that was both hardy and docile. A perfect race of a globalized world: easily bred, standardized, submissive, calibrated to statistical voracity. These specimens were smaller, they reproduced prolifically, but in doing so they diluted the primitive gene. Meanwhile, a few survivors of the wild race continued to trail their unshorn melancholy on the outermost borders. Wild yaks were the repositories of myth. From time to time, state breeders would capture a wild specimen to revitalize the domestic breeds. The fate of the drong was like a modern fable: violence, force, mystery and glory ebbing away from the earth. In the cities of the technological West, humankind, too, had been domesticated. I was well placed to describe the process; I was a perfect example. In the warmth of my apartment, a slave to my electrical ambitions, constantly recharging my screens, I had given up my lust for life.

It never snowed. Tibet extended its dry palms to heaven like death itself. That morning, at 5 a.m., we were posted at an altitude of 4,000 meters, lying behind the ridge that overlooked the cabin.

"The yaks will come," said Munier, "we're at their altitude. Every herbivore grazes at the altitude allotted to it."

The mountain was still, the air pure, the horizon clear. Where would such a herd have come from?

Silhouetted on the ridge, a sand fox basked in the sun some distance from us. Had it just come back from hunting? Hardly had I looked away than it disappeared. Lesson one: wild animals appear without warning and disappear, leaving no hope that you will ever find them again. One must be grateful for this fleeting vision, venerate it as an offering. I remembered my childhood, the all-night vigils of adoration at schools run by the De La Salle Brothers. We were required to kneel for hours, faces turned toward the chancel, filled with hope that something would happen. The brothers had vaguely indicated what it might be, but that abstract concept seemed less desirable than a football or a handful of sweets.

Beneath the vaulted ceilings of my childhood and on this Tibetan mountain ridge there reigned the same apprehension, one diffuse enough that it seemed to me benign, yet constantly present, such that it was not unnoticed: when would this wait end? There was a difference between the nave and the mountain. To kneel is to wait in expectation without proof. The prayer rises, directed to God. Will He answer? Does He even exist? Lying in a hide, the object of the wait is known. Beasts are gods that have previously appeared. Nothing disputes their existence. If something should happen, it will be a reward. If nothing happens, you break camp and resolve to start again the following day. So, if the animal appears, there will be joy. And we will welcome this companion whose existence was assured, though its visit was uncertain. The hide is a modest form of faith.

The Wolf

Toward midday, the sun was at its zenith: a pinhead in the vast emptiness. Down in the crescent-shaped valley, a forgotten cube: our hide. From our position fifty meters below the weathered ridges, we had a view of the scree-covered slopes. Munier had been right: all of a sudden, yaks appeared. They came across the pass that ringed the valley to the west. Five hundred meters away, they appeared as jade smudges scattered across the scree. They leaned against the mountain as though preventing it from falling. We needed to move toward them without making a sound, in stages, from behind, keeping upwind.

Munier and I now towered above the herd, at 4,800 meters. Suddenly the yaks scattered, scrabbling back toward the ridge whence they had come. Had they spotted our bipedal forms, the symbol of terror throughout the world? They trotted over the wine-colored slopes, looking like nothing so much as a flowing mass, moving or rather gliding like bales of wool, their hooves hidden by their chaps. When the herd reached the pass, it stopped.

"Let's keep moving along the ridge," said Munier, "we'll eventually meet up with them."

We flushed out a snowcock, and, down on the valley floor, caused a flock of Himalayan blue sheep (*Pseudois nayaur*) we had not seen arrive to retreat slowly northward. These caprids, which Munier referred to by their Hindi name *bharal*, showed off their curved horns and blue monochrome fleeces as they gamboled like chamois goats over the steep slopes. The yaks clearly considered they were safe at the altitude to which they had retreated. They did not move.

Sometime later, we had crept to within 100 meters of the herd, and were lying amid the boulders on the mountainside. I was staring at the lichen patterns on the stones: jagged flowers, like the illustrations of skin lesions in my mother's books on dermatology. Weary of such details, I looked up at the yaks. They were grazing and they too now lifted their heads. Slowly, a pair of horns rose toward the sky. They needed only to be plated in gold to become statues at the palace of Knossos. In the distance beyond the pass, wolves howled at the setting sun.

"They're singing," Munier insisted. "There are at least eight of them."

How could he possibly know? I could hear only a lone lament. Munier gave a howl. Ten minutes later, a wolf answered. So began what I think of as the most beautiful conversations between living creatures certain never to meet. "Why did we drift apart?" Munier was howling. "What do you want from me?" replied the wolf.

Munier would sing. A wolf would respond. Munier would fall silent, the wolf would start again. Then, suddenly, one of the wolves appeared on the highest pass. Munier sang a last lament and the wolf dashed down the slope heading in our direction. Having been weaned on medieval literature—the fables of the Beast of Gévaudan, the Arthurian cycle—I was not exactly thrilled to see a wolf hurtling toward us. I reassured myself by glancing at Munier, who looked about as worried as an Air France flight attendant in a pocket of turbulence.

"He'll stop dead before he gets to us," he whispered a moment before the wolf froze some fifty meters away.

It turned aside and padded in a wide circle, its muzzle turned toward us, unsettling the yaks. The herd moved further up the slopes, alarmed by the presence of the wolf. The tragedy of life in the herd: never a moment's peace. The wolf disappeared; we scanned the valley, the yaks had now reached the crest, night was drawing in; we did not see the wolf again, it had melted away.

Beauty

I n the hide, the days passed. We perfected the everyday and stuffed the cracks and holes to battle the glacial drafts. Every morning, we would leave the shack before sunrise. We felt the same agony dragging ourselves from sleeping bags in the darkness, and the same joy setting off. Fifteen minutes' exercise is enough to revive a body in a cold room. The sun came up, gilding the peaks before trickling down the slopes and eventually opening up the glacial trough, a broad avenue never carpeted by snow. Every gust of wind stirred up dust that made the air unbreathable. Over these slopes covered with loess, herds left their dotted lines of hoofprints. The stitching across the roof of the world.

Léo, Marie and I followed Munier, who followed the

animals. Sometimes, at his command, we would crouch behind the dunes and wait for the antelopes.

"Dunes" and "antelopes," Marie called them, an African bestiary.

"This country is paradise. With air conditioning."

The sun shone but afforded no warmth. The sky, a vault of crystal, weighed down the yellow air. The cold bit into us. But we stopped thinking about it when the animals came. We never saw them arrive, but suddenly they would be there, dotted through the dust. This was the apparition.

Munier told me about the first photograph he ever took, at the age of twelve: a roe deer in the Vosges. "Oh! nobility! Oh! true and simple beauty!" was the prayer offered by the young Ernest Renan as he surveyed the ruins of Athens. For Munier, that first encounter was his night spent on the Acropolis.

"That day, I shaped my destiny: to see animals. To wait for them."

Since that night, he had spent more time crouching behind bushes than sitting at school desks. His father did not force him. He never passed his baccalauréat, and earned a living working on building sites until his work as a photographer was recognized.

Scientists were scornful. Munier approached nature as an artist. His work was of little interest to statisticians, the servants of the number. I had met my fair share of number crunchers. They ringed hummingbirds and disemboweled seagulls to take samples of bile. The numbers added up. Where was the poetry? Nowhere. Did their work contribute to the sum of knowledge? Not necessarily. Science masked its limitations behind petabytes of digital data. The process of tallying the world claimed to advance science. It was pretentious.

Munier, for his part, paid tribute only to beauty. He celebrated the grace of the wolf, the elegance of the crane, the perfection of the bear. His photographs belong to art, not to mathematics.

"Your detractors would rather model the digestive system of a tiger than own a Delacroix," I told him. In the late nineteenth century, Eugène Labiche foresaw the absurdity of the age of science: "Statistics, Madame, is a modern positive science. It shines a light on the most impenetrable facts. Recently, for example, thanks to laborious research, we have managed to calculate the exact number of widows who crossed the Pont-Neuf in the year 1860."

"A yak is a lord," replied Munier. "What do I care whether he's ruminated twelve times this morning!"

Munier constantly seemed to be nurturing a melancholy. He never raised his voice for fear of startling the snowfinches.

Mediocrity

Another morning spent on the dusty slopes. The sixth. This sand had once been a mountain that was molded by rivers. These stones held secrets that stretched back. The air throttled all movement. The sky was steel blue as an anvil. Frost lay like lace over the sand. A Tibetan gazelle stood, eating snow, with delicate movements.

Suddenly, a wild donkey—a kiang—appeared. The animal stopped, warily. Munier pressed an eye to the telescopic sight. It looked almost as though he were hunting. Neither Munier nor I have the heart of a killer. Why destroy an animal more powerful and better adapted than oneself? The hunter kills twice. He kills a living creature, and, in himself, he kills the spite he feels at being less powerful than the wolf, less agile than the antelope. *Bang!* the shot rings out. "At last," says the hunter's wife.

Pity the poor hunter; it is unfair to be pot-bellied when you are surrounded by creatures as taut as a drawn bow.

The wild donkey did not leave. Had we not seen it arrive, we could have mistaken it for a statue carved from sand.

We were looking down on the bed of the frozen river, some five kilometers from our camp, and I was talking about a letter I had received some years earlier from Monsieur de B—feathered hat and velvet tailcoat—the president of the French Federation of Huntsmen, in response to an article I had written lambasting hunters. In it, he accused me of being a moccasin-wearing urbanite with no sense of tragedy, someone who strolled through gardens, maudlin about field mice and terrified by the clack of a breechblock. A pansy, I guess. As I read the letter, having just arrived back from a trek in the mountains of Afghanistan, my first thought was that it was a pity that the word "hunter" lumped together men who eviscerated woolly mammoths with spears and a gentleman with a double chin who fired grapeshot at obese pheasants between the cognac and the camembert. Using the same word to define contradictory concepts does nothing to alleviate the suffering of the world.

Life

The sterile pinpoint of the sun in its ice palace. The curious sensation of turning your face to that star and not feeling its caress. Munier continued to lead us across the glacial slopes. We never strayed more than ten kilometers from the shack. Now up toward the ridge, now down to the riverbed. This oscillation made it possible to encounter all the creatures that lived there.

The love of animals had purged Munier of all self-regard. He was not particularly interested in himself. He never complained and, consequently, we never dared say we were tired. The herbivores circle, hug the sides of the glacial valley as they graze. Small springs gush from a kink in the landscape, where the slopes meet the valley floor. A line of wild donkeys would arrive, effortlessly sure-footed, parading their fragile grace and their hides of ivory. A column of antelope would pass by, trailing a veil of dust in their wake.

"*Pantholops hodgsonii*," said Munier, accustomed to speaking Latin in the presence of animals.

Sunlight transformed the airborne dust into a shower of gold that settled as a scarlet thread. The animals' hides quivered in the light, creating the illusion of a vapor trail. Munier, a sun worshipper, always managed to find a niche that directly faced the sun. Here was a stony, desert landscape that had been thrust into the heavens by great swells of magma. The vistas we could see were the heraldic symbols of the roof of the world: a line of animals standing at the foot of a tower set on the valley floor. Every day, on these weathered plains, we saw our share of visions: raptors, pikas—the name given to Tibetan prairie dogs—sand foxes and wolves. Graceful and delicate fauna adapted to the harshness of the altitude.

On this exalted plain of life and death, a tragedy was being played out, one that was difficult to see yet perfectly regulated: the sun rose, animals chased each other to mate or to devour each other. Herbivores spent fifteen hours with their heads bowed. This was their curse: a slow life spent grazing on scant grass. For the raptors, life was more exciting. They hunted meager prey, every swoop the promise of a feast of blood, the prospect of a languorous siesta.

As animals died, the plains were scattered with the torn carcasses left by carrion feeders. Quickly, the skeletons, bleached and burned by ultraviolet light, once again became part of the whirling waltz of ecology. This was one of the great insights of ancient Greece: the world's energy as Heraclitean fire, part of a closed system, from sky to stones, from grass to flesh, from flesh to earth, under the watchful eye of the sun that offered its photons to the nitrogen cycle. The *Bardo Thodol*—the Tibetan Book of the Dead—offers a similar theory to that of Heraclitus and the philosophers of flux. Everything passes, everything flows, the wild donkeys run, the wolves hunt, the vultures hover: order, equilibrium, under the sun. A crushing silence. An unforgiving light, few men. A dream.

And here we were, in this garden at once vital, blinding and morbid. Munier had warned us: here was paradise at −30°C. Life moved in cycles: being born, running, dying, rotting, rejoining the game in some other form. I could understand the Mongol desire to leave their dead to rot on the steppes. If my mother had so wished, I would have liked us to lay her body in a valley in the Kunlun Mountains. The carrion birds would have devoured her, only to be devoured in turn by other jaws and dispersed through other bodies—rats, lammergeyers, snakes—leaving an orphaned son to imagine his mother in the beat of a wing, the ripple of snakeskin, the quiver of a fleece.

Presence

Munier made up for my myopia. His eye discerned everything, I suspected nothing. "To make the object appear, that is more important than to make it signify," Jean Baudrillard wrote on the subject of art.[*] What more can be said about antelopes? They appeared, shimmering in the distance at first, becoming more defined as they moved closer, then, suddenly, there, a presence so fragile that the slightest doubt would have dispelled. We had seen them. It was art.

Having traveled with Munier from the Vosges to Le

---

[*] Jean Baudrillard, Preface to the catalog for Charles Matton exhibition at the Palais de Tokyo, 1987.

Champsaur, Marie and Léo had made progress in the art of identifying the imperceptible. On this barren plateau, they would sometimes spot an antelope against the pale rocks, or a marmot stealing back into the shadows. To see what is unseen: a principle of Chinese Taoism and the desire of every artist. I had spent twenty-five years scouring the steppes without seeing ten percent of what Munier noticed. Oh, I had encountered a wolf in southern Tibet in 1997, I had come face-to-face with a stone marten on the roof of the Church of Saint-Maclou in Rouen, I had happened on a few bears in 2007 and in 2010 in a Siberian taiga, and even had the unpleasant experience of feeling a tarantula scuttling across my leg in Nepal in 1994, but these were accidental encounters thrust into my path; I had made no effort to seek them out. You could invest all your energy into exploring the world and go right past the living.

"I traveled around a lot, I was observed, and I was completely oblivious": this was my new psalm, one that I repeated in Tibetan fashion, in a constant hum. It summed up my life. From now on I would be aware that we were wandering amid staring eyes set in invisible faces. I counteracted my former indifference by the dual exercise of attentiveness and patience. Let us call it love.

I had just understood: the garden of humankind is filled with presences. They do not wish us ill, but they keep a close eye on us. Nothing that we do will escape their notice. Animals are the keepers of the garden where man bowls a hoop and thinks himself a king. It was a revelation. And it was not unpleasant. I knew now that I was not alone.

Séraphine de Senlis was an early twentieth-century artist who was part crazy, part genius, slightly kitsch and little appreciated. In her paintings, the trees are dotted with watchful eyes.

Hieronymus Bosch, a Flemish artist of the otherworld, titled one of his drawings *The Trees Have Ears and the Field Has Eyes.* He drew eyes embedded in the ground and propped human ears on the edges of the forest. Artists know: unbeknownst to you, the wild is watching. It disappears when the human eye perceives it.

"Over there, on that mound, a fox, about a hundred meters away," Munier would say as we were crossing the frozen river. And it would take me a long time to see what I was looking at. I did not realize that my eye had already captured what my mind refused to see. Suddenly, the animal would appear as though, pigment by pigment, detail by detail, it was taking shape amid the rocks, revealing itself to me.

I took comfort in my ineptitude. There was a pleasure in knowing one was being observed yet suspecting nothing. A fragment of Heraclitus: "Nature loves to conceal itself." What was meant by this enigma? Did nature hide itself to avoid being devoured? Did it hide itself because power has no need to manifest itself? Not everything was created by the human gaze. The infinitely small escapes our reason, the infinitely great our voraciousness, and wild animals escape our notice. Animals reign and, just as Cardinal Richelieu spied on his people, they are watching us. I knew they were alive, moving through the labyrinth. And this good news was my rejuvenation!

Simplicity

One evening, we were drinking black tea in the doorway of our shack when Marie pointed to a veil, whirling and eddying at the lowest point of the pediplain. A herd of eight wild donkeys was racing along the river, some four kilometers from the shack, coming from the east and heading toward us. Munier already had his telescope out.

"*Equus kiang*," he said when I asked him for the scientific name, kiangs to their friends.

They had stopped in a pasture of wild grasses to the north. That day we had barely seen a living creature in the valley.

The wolf that had sung the night before had spread panic. When the wolf sings, the animals don't dance. They go to ground.

Leaving the shelter, we approached the donkeys in single file, screened by an alluvial embankment. A golden eagle circled the herd. We came to a ravine carved into the slope and, crouching low in our camouflage outfits, we followed the dry riverbed. The wild donkeys were grazing nervously. Their chestnut coats with black dorsal stripes created a glorious patchwork:

"Porcelain figures on a dresser," said Léo.

Kiangs, though related to horses, had never suffered the indignity of domestication, but half a century earlier, the Chinese army had slaughtered them by the thousands to feed the troops. These were the survivors. We could make out their convex noses, their bushy manes, their rounded croups. Behind them, the wind suspended a backcloth of dust. The animals were 100 meters away and Munier had them in his sights. Suddenly, they took off westward, as though electrocuted. Our feet had dislodged a stone. An electrical tension shot across the plain. The wind gusted, light exploded in the dust clouds raised by the galloping hooves, the herd startled flights of snowfinches, a panicked fox made a frantic escape. Life, death, power, flight: beauty short-circuited.

Munier, dolefully: "My one dream in life would be to be completely invisible."

Most of my kind, including and especially myself, wanted the reverse: to be seen. We had no chance of getting close to an animal.

We retraced our steps to the cabin, not troubling to try to hide ourselves. In the gathering darkness, the cold no longer drilled into my bones, since night made it more acceptable. I closed the door of the hide, Léo fired up the gas stove, I thought about the animals. They were steeling themselves for hours of blood and ice. Outside, the night of the hunter was beginning. Already, there came the querulous screech of the owl, the bird of night. Initiating the campaign of general evisceration. Each species sought out its prey. The wolves, the lynxes, the martens prepared to launch their attacks, and the barbarous festivities would carry on till dawn when the sun put an end to the orgiastic feast. Then, the lucky carnivores would rest, their bellies full, reveling in the light that followed darkness. Meanwhile, the herbivores would once again begin their wanderings, snatching tufts of grass to convert into the energy needed to flee. Compelled by necessity to spend their lives with heads bowed toward the ground, grazing on meager sustenance, shoulders sagging beneath the yoke of determinism, cortex pressed against the frontal bone, unable to escape the cycle dooming them to sacrifice.

In the fold, we made soup. The hum of the gas stove created the illusion of heat. It was −10°C inside. We enumerated the visions of the week, headlines that were less terrible but no less fascinating than the Turkish invasion of Kurdistan. After all, a wolf attacking a herd of yaks, a golden eagle circling eight stampeding wild donkeys were scarcely less important events than a meeting between an American and his Korean counterpart. I dreamed of a daily newspaper devoted to the lives of animals. Instead of MURDEROUS ATTACK DURING CARNIVAL, we could read headlines like BLUE SHEEP REACH KUNLUN MOUNTAINS. Much dread would be lost and much poetry gained.

Munier lapped his soup and, unfailingly, with the air of a Belarusian steel worker beneath his shapka, his cheeks sunken from exertion, said in a man-of-the-world tone: "Why don't we conclude the evening on a sweeter note?" before hacking open a tin of preserves with a hunting knife. He devoted his life to the admiration of animals. Marie had started out on that path. How would they deal with going back to the world of men, in other words, to chaos?

Order

The following morning, Léo and I hid behind the alluvial bank next to the river where it was joined by one of many small tributaries. It made for an excellent hide. Dark shadows raced across the rocks. Sepulchral landscape, silent sun, blazing light. Munier and Marie were west of us, sheltering behind great black boulders. Two hundred meters away, antelopes were grazing on tufts of grass. They worked delicately, too busy at their task to know that a wolf was approaching. A hunt was about to begin, and blood would spill over the white dust.

What had happened? Why these cruel killings, this never-ending suffering? Life seemed to me to be an unending series of attacks, and the landscape, apparently unchanging, a backdrop to murders perpetrated at every level of biology from paramecia to golden eagles. Buddhism, one of the most morbid philosophies on the truth of suffering, found its perch on the Tibetan plains in the eighth century. Tibet was the perfect place to reflect upon such questions. Munier was lying in wait, he could remain in that position for eight hours. This left ample time for metaphysics.

Preliminary question: why, when I looked at a landscape, did I always see the horror behind the scenes? Even in Belle-Île, gazing at a sea softened by the sunset, at the holidaymakers eager to drink their wine before twilight, I imagined the war beneath the surface: the crabs dismembering their prey, the mouths of lampreys sucking in their victims, each fish searching out one smaller and weaker, the spines, the spikes, teeth ripping at flesh. Why not take pleasure in a scene without imagining the crime?

In an age that cannot be conceived, before the Big Bang, there existed a magnificent, monomorphic force. Its power pulsated. All around, nothingness. Humans vied with each other to give a name to this signal. To some it was God, and contained our destinies in the palm of His hand. More prudent minds called it "Being." For others it was the pulse of the primordial Om, a potential matter-energy, a mathematical point, a single undifferentiated force. The Greeks—seafarers on marble islands—called this primal pulse *kaos*. Christians—a tribe descended from sun-scorched nomads—called it "the

Word," which the Greeks translated as *pneuma*—"breath." Every people found a term to designate this oneness. And every people sharpened their swords to kill all those who contradicted them. Yet all of these propositions meant the same thing: a primal singularity pulsed through space-time. It was freed by an explosion. And so the furled became unfurled, the ineffable detailed, the unalterable ordered, the undifferentiated assumed multiple faces, the darkness was made light. This was the rupture. The end of the Unicity.

Biochemical data bubbled in the soup. Life appeared and began its conquest of the earth. Time did battle with space. This brought complication. Creatures branched out, specialized, became more distant from one another, each relying for survival on devouring others. Evolution devised sophisticated forms of predation, reproduction and locomotion. Hunting, trapping, killing and procreating was the general rule. It was open war, and the whole world was the battleground. The sun had long since caught fire. It used its own photons to fuel this butchery, dying as it sacrificed itself. "Life" was the name given to the massacre, and the requiem of the sun. If a God truly were the cause of this carnival, a supreme court should have been convened to bring Him to justice. Endowing creatures with a nervous system was the consummate invention of perversity. It consecrated pain as a principle. If God existed, His name was "suffering."

Yesterday, humankind appeared and spread like fungus.

His cortex afforded him a novel predisposition: the ability to take to the extreme the ability to destroy everything that is not himself while bewailing the fact that he is capable of doing so. Pain was joined by lucidity. Horror, perfected.

Consequently, every living being is a shard from the original stained-glass window. That morning, in central Tibet, the antelopes, lammergeyers and crickets in this war seemed to me like the facets of the disco ball suspended from the ceiling of the expanding universe. These creatures being photographed by my friends were the diffracted expression of separation. What power had ordered the invention of these forms that, with the passing of millions of years, were monstrously sophisticated, increasingly ingenious and ever more distant? The helix, the jaw, the feather and the scale, the sucker and the opposable thumb were treasures from the cabinet of curiosities of that brilliant yet deranged power that had triumphed over unity and orchestrated efflorescence.

The wolf slinked closer to the antelopes. As one, they raised their heads. Half an hour passed. Nothing moved. Not the sun, not the animals, not us, turned to stone as we peered through our binoculars. Time passed. Nothing but slow-gliding scraps of shadow storming the mountains: clouds.

Now was the reign of living beings, properties of what had been the Unicity. Evolution continued its maneuverings. Many of us dreamed of the primordial ages when everything was contained within the pulse of beginnings.

How could we appease this nostalgia for the great unmooring? We might pray to God. It was a pleasant occupation, less taxing than fishing for marlin. We addressed our thoughts to a unitary power that preceded the rupture, we knelt in a church and whispered psalms, all the while thinking: God, why could You not be happy simply being Yourself, rather than indulging in these biological experiments? Prayer was doomed to failure because the source had become too complex and we had come too late. Novalis put it more succinctly: "Everywhere we seek the Absolute, and always we find only things."*

Alternatively, we might believe that a residual primordial energy pulsed through each of us. In other words, that something of the original tremolo still resonated in all of us. Death would somehow fold us back into the poem. As he held a small Precambrian fossil in the hollow of his hand, Ernst Jünger mused on the emergence of life (the emergence of suffering) and dreamed of the origins: "One day, we will know that we have known each other."†

Lastly, there was Munier's approach: seek everywhere for echoes of the original score, sing with wolves, photograph cranes, use the camera shutter to reassemble the shards of the parent matter exploded by evolution. Each animal was a

---

* Novalis: *Pollen* (*Blüthenstaub*).
† Ernst Jünger, *Diaries 1945–48*.

glimmer of the lost source. Appeasing, for an instant, our sadness at no longer palpitating in the sleep of the medusa-goddess.

To lie in wait was to pray. In watching the animal, we were doing as the mystics did: saluting the primal memory. Art shared the same purpose: to piece together the fragments of the absolute. In galleries, people strolled past paintings, all tiles in a single mosaic.

I was explaining these thoughts to Léo, who took advantage of a slight rise in temperature to fall asleep. It was −15°C, the wolf began to move again, it padded away without troubling the antelopes.

PART TWO

The Parvis

The Evolution of Spaces

On the tenth day, at dawn, we left our hide and drove west in the jeeps. The sun bleached the earth. "The heart of luminous shadows," an adept of the Tao would say. We were heading toward Lake Yaniugol at the foot of the Kunlun Mountains, 100 kilometers from our shelter. Munier had said, "Let's go to the head of the valley. There'll be yaks there." A fine itinerary for the day.

It took a whole day to cover 100 kilometers of rutted track. The black slopes, worn smooth by a million winters, spilled from the heavens. The valley opened wide, sheltered by the piedmont border to the north. From time to time, a 6,000-meter peak made an appearance. Who troubled to think about them? The animals did not scale them, mountaineering did not exist around here. The gods had withdrawn. Deep crevices clawed the slopes, as though water refused to fall, that is, to die. It was −20°C, the wilderness was stirred by convergent lines: wild donkeys racing through the dust, antelopes setting world records. The animals never tired. Raptors hovered over the burrows of rodents. Golden eagles, saker falcons, blue sheep coexisted: a medieval bestiary in the frozen lands. A prowling wolf sat by the roadside on an alluvial mound looking uneasy. It was infuriating to find these animals frolicking at an altitude of 5,000 meters. My lungs were on fire.

The landscape laid down its strata like Tibetan Buddhist wall paintings to be found in monasteries. Its splendor comprised three layers. Above, the eternal snows. On the slopes, the rocks wreathed in mist. In the valley, creatures intoxicated by speed. After ten days, encountering such animals now seemed commonplace. I resented myself for growing accustomed to these apparitions. I pictured Karen Blixen nonchalantly taking breakfast every morning at the foot of the Ngong Hills, heedless of the explosions of pink flamingos. I wondered whether she had grown weary of the splendor. She had written *Out of Africa*, the most beautiful book ever written about earthly paradise. Proof that one never tires of the indescribable.

We were approaching Changtang, the prelude to my romantic rendezvous. I had been circling this bastion for years. Between the ages of twenty and twenty-five, I had traversed the peripheries, on foot, by truck, by bicycle, without ever venturing in, without even glancing over the ramparts. Occupying the heart of Tibet, at an average altitude of 5,000 meters, this plateau the size of France, peppered with deep gorges, bridged the Kunlun Mountains to the north and the Himalayas to the south. The zone was exempt from *spatial planning*, the name given by the technostructure to the destruction of spaces. The terrain was uninhabited, and traversed only by a few nomads. No towns, no roads, canvas tents clacking in the wind: this was the only human presence. Geographers had vaguely mapped this high desert plateau, retracing the fleeting journeys made by nineteenth-century explorers onto twenty-first-century maps. It might have been useful to indicate the existence of this plateau to those souls who bleat about the "end of adventure." The dead souls who whine, "We were born too late into a world with no remaining secrets." For those who are willing to look, there are shadowy regions still. You need only push open the right doors to find the hidden staircases. Changtang offered such a vista. But what an effort was involved merely to reach it.

The American biologist George B. Schaller—worldwide recognition and the buff looks of a U.S. marine—had explored the region in the 1980s, studying the fauna of bears, antelopes and leopards. He had alerted government authorities to the presence of poachers. Wildlife on the plateau was being decimated by hunting and trapping. The authorities were complicit in this slaughter. No one paid the American any heed. The region was not classified as a nature reserve until 1993, and hunting there was not banned until 2000. Schaller's book *Wildlife of the Tibetan Steppe* was our bible and took pride of place on the dashboard of the jeep. Munier had met Schaller some years earlier. The master had complimented him on his photographs of Arctic wolves. Our friend felt as though he had been knighted by a king.

For this journey, we had doubly named Schaller as our mentor. He had unearthed the mysteries of Changtang, but more than that, in the 1970s, he had walked the Dolpo district of Nepal with the writer Peter Matthiessen. The two Americans had set off in search of blue bharals and snow leopards. Schaller had sighted the snow leopard, but it had eluded Matthiessen, who had written *The Snow Leopard*, a labyrinthine book that dealt variously with tantric Buddhism and the evolution of species. Matthiessen's chief preoccupation was himself. With Munier, I was beginning to understand that in the contemplation of animals one is confronted with an inverted image of the self. Animals embody sensual pleasure, liberty, autonomy: all the things that we have given up.

Some fifty kilometers from the lake, there was a luminous

patch of sky: it was here that the body of water reflected its light. I opened the gospel according to Schaller and identified Tibetan antelopes. The caption gave the Tibetan name *Chiru*.

"Stop," said Munier, who had no need of Schaller's enlightenment.

We left the vehicles in the middle of the road. The antelopes' coats dappled the arid plain with splashes of color. A stippled gray white, and softer than cashmere, it was their fleece that had doomed them. Poachers sold their hides to the global textile industry. Despite various governmental protection programs, the species was threatened with extinction. Sunlight haloed their necks, and I could not rid myself of a thought: one of the indications of humanity's presence on earth has been our capacity to make a clean sweep. The human animal had resolved the philosophical question surrounding the definition of his nature: he was a destroyer.

So, I thought, with the eyepieces of the binoculars pressed into my sockets, the wool of these animals is destined to wind up draped over the shoulders of human beings whose physical abilities are manifestly inferior. In other words, Sophie, who cannot run 100 meters to save her life, will not blush at the thought of wearing a chiru scarf.

I was lying in the ditch by the roadside, staring across a plain strewn with white stones, Marie was filming two fencing males. Their horns clinked, the sound of porcelain against lacquered wood. Chirus have horns that curve forward, capable of piercing a belly, but could not shatter a skull. The two musketeers disengaged their foils. The victor ran toward a herd of females, his reward. Marie put the camera away:

"Same old story: they fight and then go see the girls."

The One and the Multiple

Lake Yaniugol, one of the high places of the Chinese Tao, hovered at an altitude of 4,800 meters in the middle of the steppe. It settled like a sacred host of jade upon the sand. It appeared to us at twilight, in the hollow of a ledge, flanked to the north by the sharp incisors of the Kunlun peaks soaring to 6,000 meters, and to the south by the Changtang. Behind this shimmering disk, the secret plateau.

We called the body of water the "lake of the Tao." Pilgrims flocked here every summer. They came to worship the idea of primordial oneness. Some claimed to be adepts of *Wu Wei*, the art of non-doing. The Tao was an incursion of ancient Chinese wisdom into a land suffused with Buddhist faith. The first enjoined lack of action, the second lack of desire. But what the hell were Westerners like us doing here?

Beginning in the sixth century BCE, Taoism spread its wings and came to perch on the plains of Tibet. Who brought it to these barren places? Lao Tzu riding an ox, leaving civilization after setting down the texts of the *Tao Te Ching*. I could still picture his ghost making its way through the crepuscular light of the twenty-first century.

On the western shores of the lake, the Chinese authorities had built groups of huts to shelter the pilgrims. There was not a soul and, abandoned to the whistling wind, the corrugated iron panels clacked and clanged. Red flags fluttered; a bird of prey glided across the sky. The air was empty, life constrained. Darkness fell. Even in the gathering shadows the waters were lactescent.

We set up our sleeping bags in the huts, effectively refrigerated by their metal walls. At 7 p.m., we kicked the ramshackle door closed. In the half-light, antelopes ran, pikas hopped and vultures circled.

"Carrying body and soul and embracing the one, can you avoid separation?" asks Chapter 10 of the *Tao Te Ching*. This question proved an excellent soporific. I encapsulated what had obsessed me since we first encountered the animals. Memory from a primitive force radiated throughout the world, splintering into a multitude of sadistic pieces. The source had been fragmented, something had happened. We would never know what. Was the Tao the name of the beginning, or the name of the multiplicity? I opened the first page:

> *Nameless: the origin of heaven and earth;*
> *Naming: the mother of ten thousand things;*

The origin and the beings. The absolute and the things.

Mystics looked for a mother. Zoologists interested themselves in the descendants.

Tomorrow, we would pretend to be the latter.

Instinct and Reason

An anonymous peak rose to the south. We had spotted it when we first arrived at the lake: a pyramid floating above the plateau, on the fringes of Changtang. The day after we arrived on the shores of the lake, we set off, single file, trekking through the glacis toward the eminence. We expected to reach the peak within two days. According to the map, it rose to 5,200 meters. From the summit, the view would take in the whole horizon; "It'll be our ringside seat," said Léo. This was all we wanted: a balcony overlooking the vastness. We were acting out a Taoist play: climbing into the heavens in order to observe the void. First, we had to cross a frozen river, our boots crunching across the glassy surface. Having reached the far shore, we began our ascent of the scree-covered slopes.

Munier, Marie and Léo trudged on, weighed down by Sherpas' loads. The provisions, the bivouac, not to mention the photographic equipment, meant that my friends were carrying thirty-five kilos. Munier was lugging forty kilos. And he refused to abandon his cultural baggage, the weighty tome by Schaller. I had misgivings about not contributing to the collective effort. I compensated for my shame by taking notes which I read out to my companions when we stopped. The ink froze in the pen, I scribbled quick sentences: "The slopes are streaked with black veins, spilled from the inkwell of some God who set down his quill after writing the world." I swear that these were not exaggerated images, because the detrital cones at 5,000 meters looked like inkwells placed on a desk, their sides spattered with a patina of jade. In the far distance, suspended yaks provided the punctuation.

The scree covered the dark slopes with a bronze armor. The patina was a reflection of the air that we breathed. We trekked on, blinded by the cold and cleansed by the wind. My companions would sit for a moment on a stepped terrace to catch their breath. Ravines opened up dark corridors. They beckoned three races: the thinker, the prospector, the hunter. We were of the first. Each valley called to us, but we did not turn from our goal. In the afternoon, we pitched camp at 4,800 meters in the hollow of an arid valley and, before it grew dark, climbed to a rocky outcrop 200 meters higher that overlooked a glacial valley. At six o'clock, a single yak stepped out onto the opposite peak, a kilometer away. It was followed by a second, and a third, and soon there were twenty, appearing out of the last glimmers of light. In silhouette, their bulky frames formed the crenellations of a castle.

They were totems from down the ages. They were heavy, powerful, silent, still: they were antediluvian. They had not evolved; they had not interbred. For millions of years they had been guided by the same instincts, their desires encoded in the same genes. They stood fast against the wind, against the slope, against interbreeding, against all forms of evolution. Being stable, they remained pure. They were time machines caught in flight. Prehistory wept, and each tear was a yak. Their shadows said: "We are of nature, are unchanging, we are of now and always. You are of culture, malleable and unstable, you are constantly innovating, where are you headed?"

The thermometer read −20°C. We humans were fated only to pass through such places as these. Most of the surface of the earth was not suited to our race. Poorly adapted, with no specialization, our deadly weapon was our cortex. This was what made everything possible. We could bend the world to our intelligence and live in the natural habitat of our choice. Our reason compensated for our weakness. Our misfortune lay in the difficulty of choosing where to settle.

How to decide between our conflicting inclinations? We

were not creatures "devoid of instincts" as certain cultural philosophers asserted; on the contrary, we were burdened by too many contradictory instincts. Humankind suffered from genetic indetermination: the price to be paid was indecisiveness. Our genes ordained nothing; it was left to us to decide between the countless possibilities offered to our caprices. It was dizzying. The ability to encompass everything was a curse. Humankind longed to do the things he most feared, ached to transgress laws he had just created; no sooner did he come home than he dreamed of setting off on some adventure; no sooner did he set sail than he wept for Penelope. Uniquely adapted to every kind of embarkation, humankind was doomed to forever being discontented. He dreamed of "being both," but "being both" is biologically impossible, psychologically undesirable and politically untenable.

On certain nights, on a terrace of a Paris café in the fifth arrondissement, I would picture myself in a tranquil little cottage in Provence only to quickly dismiss this imagining as some grand adventure. Incapable of settling on a single direction, wavering between stillness and movement, subject to vacillation, I envied the yaks, these beasts shackled to their determinism and by the same token endowed with the contentment of being what they were, of being here where they could survive.

Among humans, the geniuses were those who chose a single path and never strayed. Hector Berlioz considered the "idée fixe" the prerequisite for genius. He subjected the quality of a work to the singularity of purpose. If one wanted to go down in history, there was no room for flitting about.

An animal, on the other hand, confined itself to the surroundings bounded by chance. Genetic coding predisposed it to survive in its biotope, however hostile. And this adaptation made it sovereign. Sovereign because devoid of the urge to be elsewhere. The animal, that idée fixe.

The temperature was plummeting, it was time to leave. We left the yaks. They ruminated, they did not move. We were masters of the world, but frail, tormented masters. We were Hamlet pacing the battlements.

We got back to the camp, crawled into our sleeping bags. Before zipping up the tents, Munier gave us a piece of advice:

"Don't put in earplugs, the wolves might sing."

It was to hear such sentences that I loved to travel.

Then the moon rose but could do nothing for us, under canvas it was −30°C. Dreams turned to ice.

The Earth and the Flesh

A t four in the morning, the alarm went off. The thermometer read −35°C. There was something profoundly rash about getting out of a sleeping bag.

In order not to suffer from the cold in such conditions meant being organized. Every movement had to correspond to a single note: find a glove, lace one's boots inside the sleeping bag, keep everything prepared, take off a mitten in order to close a strap then quickly slip it on again. The slightest delay allowed the cold to bite into a limb, and it let go only to sink its teeth into another. Cold prowled inside the body. The body did not become inured to it over time. But by making swift, precise gestures, it was possible to reduce the pain. Munier had so often folded up his tent in winters spent in Ellesmere or Kamchatka that he moved quickly and did not seem to suffer from the cold. Léo's every gesture was meticulous. He was ready before me. His rucksack strapped, his clothes wrapped tightly. Marie and I scrambled to get ready, we keenly felt the pain of waking in a cold room and were eager to set off walking. According to the *Tao*, "movement overcomes cold." This was also the premise of the first law of thermodynamics. That morning, in accordance with Chinese philosophy and thermal physics, we joyously threw ourselves into exertion.

We climbed to an altitude of 5,200 meters along broad ridges. Not being acclimatized, we moved slowly. The peak was a small platform of smooth stone cracked by the ice. Day was breaking and, from the summit, a vista unfurled of the Changtang plateau. A plain spanning 1,000 kilometers that shimmered with dust and was shot through by opalescent marshes. The horizon was the morning mist. Within this emptiness was life, concealed.

I imagined long treks from east to west. There are places whose very names conjure dreams, and Changtang did so for me. Sometimes, these magical words become the names of paintings, the titles of poems. Victor Segalen dreamed of *Thibet*, a place he never reached, one he spelled with an "h."

He saw it as an abyss in which to cleanse the soul. Later, Thibet became the title of one of his collections, a declaration of love to inaccessible places. He expressed the Germanic notion of *fernweh*, a homesickness for the far-distant he would never visit. Spread out at my feet, Changtang offered up its nothingness to future adventures: it was a kingdom to be conquered, a land to be crossed on horseback, in formation, pennants fluttering. One day, we would step directly onto its arid terrain. I was happy to have seen the plain from above. I made an appointment with a place I would never know.

We spend two hours at the summit without seeing a single animal, not even a raptor. A bleeding piece of earth marked the place where the Chinese had gouged the land with bulldozers. Prospecting for metals?

"The whole area was cleared," says Munier, "like my part of the Vosges. When I was young, back in the sixties, my father warned his fellow citizens. He foresaw disasters. Rachel Carson wrote *Silent Spring* to condemn the use of pesticides. There weren't many people back then who saw the looming threat. René Dumont, Konrad Lorenz, Robert Hainard: they were wasting their breath. My father fretted, he agonized, people called him a leftist, in the end it made him sick, cancer of despair."

"He suffered the ills of the earth in his flesh," I say.

"If you like," says Munier.

• • •

WE SPENT A DAY returning to the center of the world, our lake. Night was falling, and, after an eight-hour trek, we sat on the lake shore. The silence thrummed. The shadowy ranks of the Kunlun Mountains mounted a friendly guard. The vast plain was empty. No sound, no movement, no scent. This was the great sleep. The Tao rested, not a wrinkle stirred the lake. From its stillness, wisdom was born.

> *The ten thousand things stir about; I only watch for*
> *their going back.*
> *Things grow and grow, But each goes back to its root.*
> *Going back to the root is stillness.*

I loved this narcotic abstruseness. The Tao, like the whorls from a Havana cigar, tracing pleasing enigmas. We are not called upon to understand much, but drowsiness is as voluptuous as reading Saint Augustine.

Monotheism could never have been born in Tibet. The notion of the one God had been forged in the Fertile Crescent. A throng of crop farmers and livestock farmers converged. Along the riverbanks, small towns appeared. It was no longer enough to simply slaughter a sacrificial bull to the mother goddess. Communal life needed to be ordered, harvests celebrated, sheep led safely home. They forged an image of the world that glorified the herd, the pack. Invented a universal thought. The Tao remained the creed of a solitary soul, wandering the plains. The faith of a lone wolf.

"Read the *Tao* again!" Léo said to me.

"All things originate from Being."

No sprinting antelope came to contradict this verse.

PART THREE

The Apparition

Now, the goddess. Munier wanted to reach Zadoï, to the far east of Tibet, in the upper basin of the Mekong. From there, we would travel to the massifs that offered a refuge to the surviving snow leopards.

"Survivors of what?" I ask.

"The propagation of humankind," says Marie.

Definition of humankind: the most prosperous animal in the history of living creatures. As a species, it has no predators: it clears land, it builds, it goes forth and multiplies. And having spread, it hoards. Its cities reach toward the heavens. As a nineteenth-century German poet put it, "man dwells poetically on this earth."[*] It was a glorious idea, a naïve

---

[*] Hölderlin, from "In Lovely Blue."

dream. It never came to pass. In turn, in the twenty-first century, man dwells on the earth as a co-owner. He has won the game, he thinks of his future, on the lookout for the next planet to sop up his overflow. All too soon, the "infinite spaces" will become his waste outlet. A few millennia ago, the God of Genesis (whose sayings were set down before He fell silent) had been precise: "Be fruitful, and multiply, and replenish the earth, and subdue it" (1:28). One might reasonably assume (no disrespect to the priesthood) that this project had been accomplished. The earth "subdued," and that it was time to give the womb some respite. We were eight billion humans. There were only a few thousand snow leopards. Humanity was no longer playing fair.

Nothing but Animals

A year earlier, Munier and Léo had spent time on the far bank of the river, studying the fauna near the Buddhist monastery. The very name Mekong was enough to justify the trip. Names resonate, and we go toward them, drawn by magnetic force. Whether to Samarkand or to Ulan Bator. For others, Baalbek is enough. Some quiver at the very name of Las Vegas.

"Do you like the names of places?" I asked Munier.

"I prefer the names of animals," he said.

"Your favorite?"

"The falcon, my spirit animal. You?"

"Baikal, my favorite place."

The three of us climbed back into the jeeps and spent two days driving back through the glacial valleys by which we had come, "over the alluvial slopes of the Holocene" as my professor of geomorphology at Paris-Nanterre University would have put it. The cold air crackled. The veil lifted by the jeeps was moraine dust, ground down by glaciers and left as sedimentary deposits millions of years ago. In nature, no one ever dusts.

We breathed in flecks of scoria; the sky smelled of flint. Marie shot pictures of the sun through dust trails raised by the herds. She smiled as she contemplated the void. Léo was repairing cameras that had been jolted by the ride; he liked things to be shipshape. Munier was murmuring the names of animals.

The road to Zadoï was in ruins and we were moving at a snail's pace. Granite embankments feebly shored up the plateau. The road rose over a hill between grubby banks of névé: we were happy to get through the pass. There followed long hours of hairpin bends. The earth smelled of icy water. A land without snow, white with dust. Why did I feel such an affection for these vistas shorn of nuance, these jagged landscapes, these harsh climates? I was born in the Paris basin; my parents had introduced me to the topography of Le Touquet. Under a leaden sky in Picardy, I had visited the village where my father was born. I had been taught to love

Courbet, the gentle sweep of Thiérache and of Normandy. I was closer to Bouvard and Pécuchet than to Genghis Khan, and yet I felt at home in these glacial valleys. In the steppes of central Asia that I had often visited—Russian Turkistan, Afghan Pamir, Mongolia and Tibet—I felt as though I was pushing wide the door within me. As soon as the wind whipped up, I rediscovered my sense of the country. Two possible explanations: either I had been a Mongol stable-hand in a previous life, a metempsychotic theory supported by the blazing almond-shaped eyes of my mother. Or these arid uplands reflected my frame of mind. Being neurasthenic, I needed the steppes. Perhaps this was a geo-psychological theory worth exploring. Human beings suited their geographical tastes to their moods. The faint-hearted would favor flowery meadows, stout hearts would be drawn to marble cliffs, dark souls to the shadowy forests of Brenne, and more stalwart individuals to granite bedrock.

Just before we turned onto the tarmacked Golmud–Lhasa road, a wolf appeared. He trotted along the embankment, his neck stretched out. Without slowing his pace, he turned his head to make sure we were not moving toward him, then veered away sharply. He cut across the road, heading due north, toward the foothills. At the same instant, some one hundred wild donkeys came charging past. It was a slow ballet played out on a vast stage. Each animal moved according to a strict choreography: the wolf trotted, the donkeys galloped, they came within fifty meters of a group of Tibetan antelopes and Mongolian gazelles standing motionless in the wild rye grass. The two groups stood close together but did not mingle, while the wild donkeys raced past without troubling their calm. In the animal kingdom, species rub shoulders, they are tolerant of each other, but they are not friends. Don't jumble everything together: an excellent solution to communal living.

THE WOLF LOPED PAST the herd and headed down the glacis. Wolves can run for twenty-four kilometers at a burst. This one seemed to know where it was going. The wild donkeys had spotted it. A few glanced over their shoulder, keeping a watchful eye. None of them seemed panicked. In a fatalistic world, fatality, predators and prey necessarily cross paths, each knows each other. Herbivores are aware that one among them will one day fall victim and that this is the price to pay for grazing in the sunshine. Munier offered me a slightly less woolly explanation:

"Wolves hunt in packs, they have a strategy, they tire out their prey. But a lone wolf can't do much damage when dealing with a herd."

. . .

WE WERE APPROACHING THE upper Mekong basin. At this altitude, the river was little more than a stream. One morning, in a small yellow valley perched at the height of Mont Blanc, near a farm festooned with traditional flags, we surprised three wolves on the slope, three crooks slinking home after a heist. They padded up toward the ridge, the last of the three carrying a hunk of meat in its jaws. The farm dogs howled murderously, but did not dare run after them. Dogs are like men: fury in their mouths, fear in their bellies.

The farm owners stood on the threshold and helplessly watched the scene: "What can be done and who is to blame?" they seemed to be saying. The three wolves raced on, proud, peerless, unpunished, unassailable as the sun. They stood on the ridge and the cub devoured the hunk of flesh while the two adults stood watch, hind paws tensed, chests distended. We crept up toward them, hidden by a low bank. By the time we reached the ridge, they had vanished. An owl fluttered, a fox barked, antelopes hugged the slopes. Of the wolves, no trace.

"They've disappeared, but they can't be far off," whispered Munier.

This was a good definition of nature in the wild: what is still present when you cannot see it. We were left with the memory of three desperadoes, loping through the dawn light to the yelping of dogs before disappearing on another raid. Fifteen minutes before we arrived, the wolves had been singing, responding to a call from somewhere to the north.

"They're going to join a pack. They've got preset meeting points," said Munier. "Seeing a wolf thrills me."

"Why?"

"An echo of wilder times. I was born in overpopulated France, where power is waning and space is at a premium. In France, if a wolf kills a sheep, the farmers protest. They're out waving placards: WOLVES OUT!"

Wolves do not linger in France, the country has a taste for flocks and herds. A people that loves majorettes and banquets cannot bear to allow a master of the night to roam freely.

Already, the farmers were heading back to the farmhouse, kicking the dogs out of the way. On earth, the gazelle sprints, the wolf prowls, the yak swaggers, the vulture ponders, the antelope takes flight, the pika takes the sun and the dog pays the price for everyone.

Love on the Ice Slopes

The road had joined a tributary that snaked across the rocky plain at almost 5,000 meters. The walls of the valley bristled with limestone turrets. Caves pockmarked the defensive ramparts, sketching black tears in the façade.

"This is a kingdom for snow leopards," said Munier.

THE SHEEPFOLD WHERE HE wanted us to set up our base camp was 100 kilometers further on.

A Pallas's cat (*Otocolobus manul*) suddenly appeared on a crag above the road, its shaggy head, needle-like canines and yellow eyes radiated a demonic glare that belied its furry gentleness. This small wild cat lived at the mercy of many predators. It seemed to resent evolution for gifting it with such fierce aggression in such a cuddly body. Its rictus smile said, "Try and pet me and I'll rip your throat out." A blue sheep stood perched on a steep ridge, the curves of its horns merging with the crenellations. Beasts watched over the world, just as gargoyles stood vigil over the cities from their belfries. We passed below, oblivious to their presence. All day it was the same gymnastic display. Each time we spotted an animal, we would leap from the vehicles, crawl along the ground, point our cameras. By the time we were in place, the animals had vanished.

I didn't dare confide my conclusions to Léo, but it was obvious: Munier and Marie were in love. Silently, with no rapturous transports. Tall and statuesque, he held the keys to reading the world and recognized the mystery of this gracile woman who gave away little of herself. Taciturn and gloriously limber, she admired this man who knew many secrets, but could not unlock hers. They were two young Greek gods in the bodies of higher animals. It was a joy just to see them together, even if it was −20°C and they were crouching in a thorny thicket.

"Love is lying motionless next to each other for hours at a time," I said.

"We were made for lying in wait," Marie confirmed.

That morning, she filmed the Pallas's cat while Munier scanned the ridges to determine which little prairie dog was about to die in the gladiatorial arena.

It seemed that Munier, though revolted by the assault of humankind on nature, still harbored some affection for his own kind. He reserved these feelings for precise, formally identifiable individuals. I admired this targeted use of love. An honorable usage.

Munier, though extremely charitable, did not claim to be a humanist. He preferred the animal in the viewfinder of his binoculars to the man in the mirror and did not place the human animal at the apex of the pyramid of living creatures. He knew that the human race, only recently arrived in the terrestrial mansion, claimed to be the master and secured its glory by wiping out everything that was not itself.

My comrade-in-arms did not vow undying love to the abstract notion of humankind, but to actual beneficiaries: in effect, to animals and to Marie. Flesh, bones, hair, skin: rather than emotions, he needed something solid, something physical.

Love in the Forest

I, too, had loved someone. Love had fulfilled its function: all else had disappeared. She was a pale, warm girl who lives in the forests of Landes. We would take walks along the pathways in the evening. The pine trees planted 150 years earlier had colonized the marshland, flourished in the hinterland behind the dunes, and exuded a warm, acrid smell: the sweat of the earth. We walked effortlessly along the rubbery ribbons of the pathways. "People should live at the pace of the Sioux," she would say. We surprised animals, a bird, a roe deer. A snake slithered away. The man of antiquity—muscles of chiseled marble and vacant eyes—saw such animal appearances as the apparition of a god.

"It's injured and can't run away, she's spotted it, it's going to die." For months I heard phrases like this. That evening, it was a spider—"a wolf spider," she informed me—had come upon a longhorn beetle behind a frond of fern. "She's going to inject it with a lethal dose, she's going to devour it." Like Munier, she knew such things. Who had instilled these insights into her? It was the wisdom of the ancients. A knowledge of nature flourishes in certain creatures who have never studied it. They are seers, they perceive the intricate structure of things while scientists are focused on a single part of the edifice.

She would read the hedgerows. She understood birds and insects. When the beachgrass blossomed, she would say, "It is the orison of the flower to its god the sun." She would save ants that got swept away by a stream, snails caught in brambles, birds with broken wings. Faced with a scarab beetle, she would say: "It is a heraldic element, it deserves our respect, it is at one with nature." One day, in Paris, a sparrow landed on her head and I wondered whether I was worthy of this woman whom birds chose as a perch. She was a priestess; I followed her.

We lived in the forests at night. She had a stud farm in Landes that spanned a dozen hectares on the western slopes of a dirt track whose deep rut seemed to her the guarantee of a covert life. On the outskirts of the forest, she had built a pine cabin. A large pond was the principal axis of the property.

There, mallard ducks rested, and horses came to drink. All around, dense grasses drilled through the sand trampled by the animals. All of the comforts of the cabin: a stove, some books, a Remington 700 bolt-action rifle, all the necessities for making coffee, and an awning under which to drink it, and a tack room that smelled of pine resin. This kingdom was guarded by a sharp-eared Beauceron sheepdog, twitchy as the trigger on a Beretta 92, but friendly to those who were polite. He would have ripped the throat out of an intruder. I managed to escape with my life.

Sometimes, we would sit on the dunes. The ocean raged and pounded, while the waves crashed, indefatigable. "There must be some ancient quarrel between the sea and the land." I used to say such things, she did not listen.

Nose buried in her hair, which smelled of boxwood, I allowed her to spin out her theories. Man had appeared on earth some millions of years ago. He had arrived uninvited, after the table had been set, the forests unfurled, the beasts frolicking. The Neolithic revolution, like all revolutions, fomented the Terror. Man declared himself head of the politburo of all living things, hoisted himself to the top rung of the ladder and made up screeds of dogma to legitimize his dominion. All in defense of the same cause: himself. "Man is God's hangover!" I would say. She did not like these pronouncements. She accused me of launching damp squibs.

. . .

It was she who first introduced me to the idea I explained to Léo amid the sand dunes of Tibet. Animals, plants, single-cell life forms and the neocortex are all fractals of the same poem. She talked to me about the primordial soup: four and a half billion years ago, a principal matter had existed, churning in the waters. The whole antedated the parts. From this prebiotic broth, something emerged. A separation occurred, leading to a branching of organic forms of increasing complexity. She worshipped all living things as a shard of the mirror. She would pick up a fox's tooth, a heron's feather, a cuttlefish bone, and whisper as she contemplated each shard: "We proceed from the Same."

Kneeling in the dunes, she would say: "She is going back to find the column, she was drawn to the sap of the stonecrop, the others missed it."

This time it was an ant rejoining its column after a detour via a patch of stonecrop. Where did she get her infinite tenderness for the minutiae of animal life? "From their willingness to do things properly," she would say, "their preciseness. Humans aren't conscientious."

In summer, the sky was clear. The wind churned the sea, a cloud appeared from the eddies. The air was warm, the sea wild, the sand soft. On the beach, human bodies lay supine. French people had grown fat. Too much screen time? Since the sixties, societies had spent their lives sitting. Since the cybernetic mutation, images flickered in front of motionless bodies.

An airplane would fly past trailing a banner advertising an online dating site. "Imagine the pilot flying over the beach and seeing his wife lying next to some guy she met on that site," I would say.

She was staring at the gulls surfing the wind, riding the crest, framed by the sunlight.

We would walk back to the cabin along smooth paths. Her hair now smelled of candle wax. To her, the rustle of the trees was filled with meaning. The leaves were an alphabet. "Birds don't sing out of vanity," she would say. "They sing patriotic anthems or serenades: this is my home; I love you." We would arrive back at the cabin and she would uncork a wine from the Loire, of sands and mists. I drank greedily, the red venom swelling my veins. I could feel night welling inside me. A barn owl screeched. "I know that owl, it lives around here, the spirit of night, the commander-in-chief of dead trees." This was one of her obsessions: re-creating a classification of living creatures, not according to Linnaean taxonomy, but according to a transversal taxonomy bringing together plants and animals according to their disposition. Thus, there was the spirit of voracity (shared by sharks and the carnivorous plants), the spirit of cooperation (a quality shared by jumping spiders and kangaroos), the spirit of longevity (the hallmark of the tortoise or the sequoia), of concealment (exemplified by the chameleon and the stick insect). It did not matter that these creatures did not belong to the same biological phylum so long as they shared the same skills. Hence, she concluded, a cuckoo and a flukeworm, through their opportunism and their intimate knowledge of their victims, were more closely related to each other than to certain members of the same family. To her, the living world was a panoply of stratagems, for war, for love and for locomotion.

She would go out to stable the horses. Unhurried, clear and precise, she was a Pre-Raphaelite vision as she walked beneath the moon, followed by her cat, by a goose, by horses with no halters, by her dog. All that was missing beneath the starry vault was a leopard. They glided through the darkness, heads held high, without a rustle or a sound, without touching, perfectly aligned and perfectly distanced, knowing where they were headed. An orderly troop. The animals stirred like springs at the slightest movement by their mistress. She was a sister of Saint Francis of Assisi. If she believed in God, she would have joined an order of poverty and death, a mystical nocturnal sisterhood that communicated with God without clerical intercession. In fact, her communion with the animals was a prayer.

I lost her. She rejected me because I refused to give myself over body and soul to the love of nature. We would have lived in a demesne, in the deep forest, a cabin or a ruin, devoted to the contemplation of animals. The dream dissolved and I watched her walk away as softly as she had come, flanked by her animals, into the forest of the night. I went on my way, I traveled far and wide, leaping from plane to train, going from conference to conference, bleating (in a self-important tone) that humankind would do well to stop rushing around the globe. I rushed around the globe and each time I encountered an animal, it was her vanished face I saw. I followed her everywhere. When Munier first talked to me about the snow leopard on the banks of the Moselle, he could not know that he was suggesting that I go and find her.

If I were to encounter the animal, my only love would appear, embodied in the snow leopard. I offered up all my apparitions to her ravaged memory.

A Cat in a Gorge

Past Zadoï, the road wound through a gorge at an altitude of 4,600 meters. We arrived at the Bapo sheepfold, on the banks of the Mekong, 500 meters from the bank. Later we would dub this place the "canyon of the leopards." Three cob-walled shacks the size of beach huts guarded the entrance to a narrow fissure in the karst. The white ridges, covered by wine-colored lichen, rose to a height of 5,000 meters, and opened onto vast slopes where herds grazed. A trickle of icy water seeped through the rockface, tracing three meanders before spilling into the river. We made the twenty-minute walk to the riverbank where, every morning, domestic yaks wended their way hoping to find richer pasture than the day before.

No running water, no electricity, no central heating. The wind howled and lowed. Dogs mounted a jealous guard. Winding along the embankment, running parallel to the river, a road brought the occasional visitor. The yak farmer's jeep offered the hope of a trip to the modern world, in the form of Zadoï, fifty kilometers east.

A family of nomads spent their winters here, sovereign lords of nights that plummeted to −20°C and a herd of 200 yaks, while they waited for spring to come and the winds to subside. The sheer cliffs were a paradise for the snow leopard. The hollows afforded shelter. The yaks and the bharals offered tasty snacks. As for humans, they were none too clever. The four of us would stay here for ten days.

THE THREE CHILDREN WERE whip-thin. Their nervous energy protected them from the glacial temperatures. Gompa, six, and his two older sisters, Jisso and Dija, with their almond eyes and their white teeth, brought the herds to pasture at dawn and led them back to the camp at nightfall. They spent their days running about over the windswept plain, herding beasts six times their size. They had seen a snow leopard at least once in their ten years. In Tibetan, the snow leopard is called *sa'u*, and the kids were careful to shout the word, like an exclamation, baring their teeth, holding their fingers up to mimic the long fangs. The kind of children who are not lulled to sleep by Perrault's fairy tales. Sometimes, in the valleys of the upper Mekong, a snow leopard would snatch a child, the father told us.

Tougê, the fifty-year-old head of the family, allocated us the smallest of the three buildings. It afforded a very individual form of luxury: the door opened onto a steep cliff face where beasts prowled. The dogs had adopted us, there was a stove to heat the single room. In front of the camp, the river flowed for an hour each day when the sun was at its hottest. From time to time, the children would pay us a visit. Hours of cold, of silence, of solitude, immutable landscapes, granite skies, mineral domain, negative temperatures: days that promised unchanging permanence. We were aware of our good fortune.

Our time was divided between forced marches and hours of hibernation.

At night, we would visit the family in the neighboring shack. A shadowy warmth reigned behind the wooden door. The mother, churning butter tea, giving rhythm to the silence. In Tibet, family rooms are warm bellies that compensate for days of fine hail. A cat lay sleeping, the diluted genes of the leopard coursing through its veins: in choosing to purr in the warmth, it would never know the joy of killing a yak. Its distant relative, the lynx, still lived outdoors, preferring tempest to torpor. A gilded Buddha would glimmer in the glow of the oil lamps, and the hum in the air was sufficiently numbing that we could look at each other without saying a word. We no longer desired anything. Buddha had prevailed: his nihilism pervaded the drowsy numbness. The father would say his rosary. Time would pass. Silence was the mark of our devotion.

In the morning, we would take the road down into the canyon. Munier would station us on a rocky ledge or a ridge over the narrow gorge. Sometimes we would split into two groups; Munier would take Marie into an adjacent fold in the rock. In the distance, the Mekong braided its silvery mane. Meanwhile, we bided our time, waiting for the reason for our journey to appear, the snow leopard, or "ounce" (*Panthera uncia*) to give its more scientific name, the empress who had sworn allegiance to this canyon and whose public appearances we had come to witness.

Of Arts and Beasts

Five thousand snow leopards still survived in the world. Statistically, there were more humans wearing fur coats. The ounce inhabited central massifs, from the Pamirs in Afghanistan to eastern Tibet, from the Altai Mountains to the Himalayas. The area they inhabited corresponded to a historic map of the roof of the world. The expansion of the Mongol Empire, the psychotic incursions of Baron Ungern, the route taken by Nestorian monks through Serindia, the Soviet battles on the edge of the Union, Paul Peillot's archaeological missions to Chinese Turkistan: these shifts and movements mapped out the land of the snow leopard. Here, men had behaved with the dignity of wild cats. Munier, for his part, had been patrolling the eastern area of the zone for four years. The chances of catching a glimpse in an area a quarter the size of Eurasia were slim. Why had my friend not specialized in portrait photography, a career with a future? A billion and a half Chinese people versus 5,000 snow leopards: the guy deliberately made life difficult for himself.

The vultures came in shifts, sentinels to the requiem. The topmost ridges were first to welcome the daylight. A falcon swooped through the valley, scattering its benediction. I was mesmerized by the sentry duty of the carrion birds. They watched to see that all was well on earth: that death took its allotted share of animals and in return left provisions. Below, on the steep slopes that chamfered the gorge, the yaks grazed. Lying in the long grasses, cold, calm and watchful, Léo studied every crag through his binoculars. I was less conscientious. Patience has its limits, and I had come to the end of mine when we reached the canyon. I was busy assigning each animal a rung on the social ladder of the kingdom. The snow leopard was the regent; her status reinforced by her invisibility. She reigned, and therefore had no need to show herself. The prowling wolves were knavish princes; the yaks, richer burghers, warmly attired; the lynxes were musketeers; the foxes country squires; the blue sheep and the wild donkeys were the general populace. The raptors represented the priests, hieratic masters of the heavens and of death. These clerics in plumed livery were not against the idea that things might bode ill for us.

The canyon snaked between limestone towers pierced with caves, archways dappled with shadows. The winds positioned the clouds and regulated the albuminous light. It was a setting worthy of King Ludwig II of Bavaria, set down by a Chinese engraver with a penchant for ghosts. Blue sheep and golden foxes gliding across the slopes, through the mists, put the finishing touches to the composition. A painting created millions of years earlier by tectonic activity, biology and devastation.

The landscape was my art school. Appreciating the beauty of forms requires an education, an eye. Studying geography provided me with the keys to alluvial valleys and glacial troughs. The Louver had initiated me into the nuances of Flemish Baroque and Italian Mannerism. I did not feel that artworks made by man outshone the perfection of landscapes, nor Florentine Madonnas the grace of blue sheep. To me, Munier was more artist than photographer.

Of leopards and felines, I knew only artists' representations. *O canvases, o seasons!* In Roman times, the wild cat roamed the southern borders of the Empire and embodied the spirit of the Orient. Cleopatra and the leopard shared the title Queen of the Nile. In Volubilis, in Palmyra, in Alexandria, artists made mosaics depicting panoplies of animals in which leopards danced in Orphic circles with elephants, bears, lions, and horses. The spotted pattern—what Pliny the Elder in the first century AD called "the stippled coat"—was a mark of power and voluptuousness. Pliny claimed to know that "the sexual passions of these animals are very violent."[*] A panther passed, and already a Roman was imagining the rug on which he could cavort with a slave girl.

Eighteen hundred years later, the great cats fascinated the romantic painters. In the salons of 1830, the public of the Bourbon Restoration discovered savagery. Delacroix depicted the wild beasts of the Atlas ripping the throat from a horse. He created furious paintings of striking musculature and swirling smoke in which dust eddied despite the thick impasto. Romanticism giving classicism a slap in the face. And yet Delacroix also painted a tiger at rest, luxuriating in his strength before the carnage. The painting depicted brutality, it was a far cry from the virgins of yesteryear.

Jean-Baptiste Corot created a curiously proportioned leopard ridden by an infant Bacchus advancing on a supine woman. This strangely clumsy image reveals a masculine terror. Fearful of ambiguity, man does not like the idea of a purring monster playing with a baby and a fat Bacchante. So it must be the woman who is dangerous. You can never be too careful. Through the leopard, the artist was taking aim at the fatal faerie, the virgin in thigh boots, cruel Venus. It's well known that carnivores can devour a man, so one must beware their beauty. Alexandre Dumas' Milady is one such.

---

[*] *The Natural History of Pliny*, Book VIII.

One day, insulted by her brother-in-law, she gave a "muffled roar and backed into a corner of the room, like a panther preparing to spring."[*]

The fin-de-siècle was inspired by the legends of Melusina. In a cryptic canvas of 1896 entitled *Des Caresses*, the Belgian artist Fernand Khnopff—part dreamer, part symbolist—depicts a leopard with the head of a woman flirting with a lover who is deathly pale. One dare not imagine the young man's fate.

Some of the Pre-Raphaelites conjured wild beasts in their daubs. Scantily clad princesses or weary demigods advance toward the viewer through a saccharine glow, flanked by leopards reduced to stuffed dummies draped in mottled fur. Such painters celebrated the sheer beauty of the motif. Edmund Dulac or Briton Rivière turned it into a bedside rug on which to beach their hyper-stylized dreams.

Later, the power of the animal mesmerized the master of art nouveau. The perfection of the species was well suited to the muscular steel aesthetic. Jouve arched it like a taut bow. The leopard as a weapon. Better yet, Paul Morand's Bugatti T35B. It perfectly embodied movement, effortless, remorseless. Unlike jaguars, it did not crash into trees. Thanks to the finely honed design of Rembrandt Bugatti and Maurice Prost, the big cat emerged from the laboratory of evolution

---

[*] Alexandre Dumas, *The Three Musketeers.*

to be worthy of crouching at the feet of a 1930s brunette holding a glass of champagne in front of her small, pert breasts.

Within 100 years, leopard print would appear on handbags, on wallpaper in Palavas-les-Flots. Every age has its own style of elegance, every epoch does what it can. Our era sunbathed in its underwear.

Munier was not indifferent to the profitability of the animal in the arts. He drummed up support for big cats. Dreary minds reproached our friend for celebrating only pure beauty. In an age of anxiety and morality, it was considered a crime. "What about the message," they said, "and the melting ice-caps?" In Munier's books, wolves floated in the empty Arctic wastes, Japanese cranes tangled in their courtship dances, and bears as light as snowflakes disappeared behind tufts of mist. There were no turtles suffocated by plastic bags, nothing but animals in all their beauty. It was almost possible to imagine oneself in the Garden of Eden. "People resent me for favoring the aesthetic of the animal kingdom," he defended himself. "But we've already got enough witnesses to disaster! I seek out beauty, I pay homage to it. This is my way of defending it."

Every morning, in the valley, we waited for beauty to descend from the Elysian Fields.

The First Apparition

We knew that the leopard was prowling. Sometimes I would catch a glimpse: it was only a rock; it was only a cloud. I lived in expectation. During the months he spent in Nepal in 1973, Peter Matthiessen did not get to see a snow leopard. To those who asked whether he had seen it, he would say, "No! Isn't that wonderful?"[*] Well, no, my dear Peter. It's not "wonderful." I could not understand how anyone could make a virtue of disappointment. It was intellectual sleight of hand. I wanted to see the snow leopard, that was why I had come. Because its appearance would be my offering to the woman from

---

[*] Peter Matthiessen, *The Snow Leopard*.

whom I was separated. And even if, out of politeness, which is to say my hypocrisy, I told Munier that I had gone with him simply because I admired his photography, I longed to see a snow leopard. I had my reasons; they were personal.

Ceaselessly, my friends scanned the landscape with their telescopes. Munier could spend a whole day studying the slopes, centimeter by centimeter. "All I need is to see a trace of urine on a rock," he would say. On the second night in the canyon, we were heading back to the Tibetan camp when we encountered it. The sky still gave off a faint glow. Munier spotted it, about 500 meters due south of us. He handed me the telescope and precisely indicated where I should look, but even then it was a long moment before I could make it out, meaning before I could grasp what it was that I was looking at. Though the animal was a simple, massive living form, it was a shape that was utterly unknown to me. And the mind requires some time to accept something that is unfamiliar. The eye receives the image crystal clear but the mind refuses to acknowledge it.

The snow leopard was resting, lying at the foot of a rocky outcrop already dappled by shadows, half-hidden by bushes. A hundred meters further down the slope, the river ran through the gorge. We could have walked within a few paces of it without ever noticing. It was a religious apparition. Even now, the memory of that vision is imbued with an otherworldly sanctity.

The snow leopard lifted its head, sniffed the air. It was garbed in the heraldry of the Tibetan landscape. Its coat, a mosaic of gold and bronze, belonged to day, to night, to heaven and to earth. It had taken the ridges, the névés, the shadows of the canyon and the crystal of the sky, the autumnal slopes and the eternal snows, the spikes of the sagebrush, the secret of the storms and clouds of silver, the gold of the steppes and the shroud of the ice, the death of the mountain sheep and the blood of the cattle chamois. It lived beneath the fleece of the world. It was robed in representations. This animal, the spirit of the snows, had clothed itself with the earth.

I thought the leopard was camouflaged to blend with the landscape, but it was the landscape that vanished when it appeared. By an optical effect like a dolly zoom in cinema, every time my eye alighted on the leopard, the background receded and everything was reduced to the features of its face. Born of this substratum, the snow leopard had become the mountain, had emerged from it. The snow leopard was there and the whole world had vanished. The animal incarnated the Greek *physis*, the Latin *natura*, for which Heidegger offered the numinous definition "that which emerges and, as emerging, abides."*

In short, a stippled big cat sprang from nothingness to take up the whole landscape.

---

* Martin Heidegger, *Remarques sur Art-Sculpture-Espace.*

We stayed then until darkness was complete. The snow leopard dozed, immune to all threats. Other animals seemed like wretched, fearful creatures. A horse bolts at the slightest movement, a cat at the slightest sound, a dog detects an unfamiliar smell and jumps to its feet, an insect takes shelter, a herbivore dreads hearing something move behind it, even the human animal instinctively checks the corners when entering a room. Paranoia is an occupational hazard of living. But the leopard was confident of its absolutism. It dozed, utterly abandoned, since it was untouchable.

Through the binoculars, I saw it stretch. It lay back down. It was the ruler of its life. It was the expression of this place. Its mere presence signified its "power." The world was its throne, it filled the space it inhabited. It incarnated that mysterious concept of the king's body. A true regent is content simply to be. He does not trouble to act, and sees no need to make appearances. His existence is the foundation of his authority. The president of a democracy, on the other hand, must constantly be seen, like a traffic cop at a roundabout.

Fifty meters away, the yaks continued to graze, unruffled. They were content because they did not know their predator was skulking among the rocks. Psychologically, no prey could endure the knowledge that it lives cheek by jowl with death. Life is livable if the threat is ignored. Creatures are born with their own blinkers.

Munier handed me the most powerful telescope. I gazed

at the animal until my eye dried out from the cold. The features of the face sloped toward the muzzle, sketching lines of force. It turned to face me. Its eyes bored into me. Two blazing, glacial orbs of scorn. It got to its feet and stretched its neck toward us. "It's spotted us," I thought. "What will it do? Pounce?"

It yawned.

This is the effect of man on the snow leopard of Tibet.

It turned its back, stretched again and disappeared.

I returned the telescope to Munier. It was the most glorious day of my life since my death.

"This valley is not the same now that we've seen the snow leopard," said Munier.

He, too, was a royalist, he believed in the consecration of places by the presence of the Being. We walked back down through the darkness. I had waited for this vision; it had come. Henceforth, nothing would ever be the same in this place made fruitful by the presence. Not even in my innermost self.

Lying in Wait in Space-Time

Since then, every morning we have scaled the heights of the valley, never straying further than six kilometers from the Tibetan encampment. We knew that the snow leopard was here, we might see it again. We spent the days scouring the ridges, expending as much energy as hunters on safari. We walked, we looked for tracks, we lay in wait. Sometimes we split into two groups and used radios to communicate the results of our searches. We were alert to the smallest movement. A fluttering bird's wing was enough.

"Last year," says Munier, "I gave up hope of seeing the snow leopard. I was packing away my hide when a huge crow up on the ridge sounded the alert. I stopped and watched, and suddenly, the leopard appeared. The crow had signaled to me."

"What warped mindset leads someone to put a bullet in the head of such a creature?" says Marie.

"According to hunters, it's their 'love of nature,'" says Munier.

"Should we allow hunters into art galleries?" I say. "They would slash a Velázquez for the love of art. Though, curiously, not many of them put a bullet in their brains for love of themselves."

In just one of these days, we had amassed hundreds of visions for Marie's lenses, Munier's plates, for our eyes, our personal memories, our edification. For our salvation, perhaps? The first to see an animal signaled to the others. From the moment we spotted it, a peace would well up in us, we were electrified by shock. Excitement and plenitude, contradictory emotions. To encounter an animal is an elixir of life. The eye perceives a shimmering. The animal is the key, it opens a door. Behind it, the inexpressible.

These hours spent watching were diametrically opposed to my habitual rhythms as a traveler. In Paris, I feverishly sought out random passions. "Our hurried lives,"* to quote a poet. Here, in the canyon, we scanned the landscape with no

---

* Charles Dantzig, poet and novelist.

guarantee of reward. We waited in silence for a shadow, staring into the void. It was the antithesis of an advertising slogan: we endure the cold with no certainty of a result. The modern frenzy of "everything, right now" was pitted against the "probably nothing, ever" of lying in wait. This luxury of spending a day waiting for the improbable.

I vowed that, when I went back to France, I would carry on this practice of watching from hides. No need to be in the Himalayas at an altitude of 5,000 meters. The greatness of this exercise that could be practiced anywhere was in always granting what was demanded of it. From a bedroom widow, on the terrace of a café, in a forest or by the waterside, in company or alone on a bench, it was enough to open your eyes wide and wait for something to appear. Something you would never have noticed had you not been on the lookout. And if nothing should happen, the quality of the passing time was enhanced by the focused attention. Watching and waiting was a modus operandi. It needed to become a way of life.

KNOWING HOW TO DISAPPEAR was an art. One that Munier had spent thirty years practicing, one that combined self-annulment with obliviousness to all else. He had asked that time afford him what the traveler asks of the journey: a *raison d'être*.

You lie in wait; space no longer flashes past. Time imposes its nuances with light strokes. An animal materializes. This is the apparition. The wait has been fruitful.

My friend had waited for the appearance of Lapland musk oxen, Arctic wolves, Ellesmere Island bears, Japanese cranes. He had allowed his toes to freeze in the snow, waiting day and night, faithful to a sniper's directives: scorn pain, ignore time, never give in to tiredness, never doubt the result, never retreat until you have achieved your objective.

In the forests of Karelia, elite Finnish sharpshooters kept the Soviet army at bay during the Winter War of 1939–40 despite being outnumbered. They applied the techniques of hunting in the freezing forest to waging war. A handful of them melted into the taiga where they lay in wait for the Bolsheviks at temperatures of −30°C, fingers on the triggers of their peerless M28 Mosin–Nagant rifles. They chewed snow to avoid exhaling water vapor. They would creep through the forest, find another hide, put a bullet in the head of a Russian tank driver, disappear, fire again, agile, undetectable, furtive and therefore highly dangerous.

The most famous of them, Simo Häyhä, a soldier barely five feet two, killed more than 500 Russians in the icy forests. The Red Army nicknamed him "The White Death." One day, he was picked off by a Soviet sniper. The explosive bullet from the Mosin–Nagant 91/30 ripped away his upper jaw and much of his lower jaw but, though permanently maimed, he survived.

The Finnish snipers claimed to be relaxed, resilient, relentless: the virtues of icy monsters. They were living embodiments of *sisu*. In Finnish, the word *sisu* describes the combined qualities of determination and resistance. How could we translate the term? "Spiritual abnegation," "self-effacement," "mental resistance"? In the litany of human heroism, ever since Captain Ahab set out to hunt the great white whale, the sniper has been the perfect embodiment of man fixated by a single goal.

Munier was as patient, as invisible as a Finnish sniper. He too was imbued with *sisu*. But he did not kill anyone, did not hate anyone, and, as yet, no communist had ever fired on him.

In the French army, the 13th Parachute Dragoon Regiment has mastered the art of camouflage. The dragoons infiltrate hostile territory in order to spy on enemy movements. They blend into the background, leave no trace, exude no smell, spend days on end in position. Dressed in fatigues, his camera lenses wrapped in scraps of khaki, Munier looked like one of these tree-men, rock-men, wall-men. There was, however, one notable difference: Tibetan snow leopards and Arctic wolves have more keenly developed sensory equipment than murderous terrorists.

Sometimes, while practicing *sisu*, lying next to Munier, I

daydreamed: I imagined a dragoon parachutist crouched, camouflaged, in a forest glade. A couple of lovers appear, thrilled to have finally found an isolated spot. The gentleman lays the lady over the parachutist, who is camouflaged as a rock. What a fate for a special reconnaissance agent! Creeping through the hills to flush out state secrets only to stumble on Maurice groping Marceline. Munier never told me any stories, but I suspected that he had been witness to such fumblings.

For the moment, time passed, and time alone. A lammergeyer might circle, in the hope that we were dead. A wolf trotted past, a brazen shadow. Once, a crow passed, a torment in the memory of the sky. On another occasion, a Pallas's cat poked its head out of its bolthole, charming and affronted. Our desire to stroke it seemed to make it angry. We spent three whole days scouring the valley. The snow leopard could be a rock, and each rock could be a snow leopard, it was essential to be meticulous. I thought I saw it everywhere: on a patch of grass, behind a boulder, in the shadows. I was overwhelmed by the idea of the snow leopard. It is a common psychological phenomenon: you are obsessed with a creature; you see it everywhere. This is why men who are deeply enamored of one woman will love all others, seeking to worship the same essence in a variety of manifestations. Try telling the wife who has just caught you *in flagrante*, "Darling, it was you that I loved in all of them!"

The Pact of Surrender

The day done, we prepared to break cover. The Mekong lay lifeless, the flank of a dead fish electrified by cold. The sun was setting, the meanders aluminum, the dark was rising, touching the ridges, extinguishing the peaks one by one. A few summits—the highest—still glittered. The temperature was fast plummeting. This was the great mercy of cold and death. Who gave a thought to the struggles of the animals in the darkness? Had they all found a shelter to endure the −35°C cold? We were heading back to the warmth.

"The call of the mild," I shouted to Léo.

In half an hour we would be holding cups of tea. What was there to complain about?

At the same time, the domestic yaks were being herded back into their huts. Like farm animals, we were led by our bellies. Despite our high opinion of ourselves, humankind is ruled by soup. As we descended the slopes toward the motionless river, I recalled my mother's funeral. That day in May, we were bewildered she had died without a fight. No one had been prepared for the inevitable. During the Melkite Greek Catholic ceremony, as her coffin rested in front of the iconostasis, some of us were thinking that life now would be unbearable, that the obscenity of death would carry us in its wake. But the hours passed and, suddenly, we felt hungry. And so the assembled company, bathed in tears and believing they were inconsolable, found themselves sitting down around a table in a Greek restaurant munching grilled fish and sipping retsina. The gastric glands are more imperious than their lacrimal counterparts, and, that day, it seemed to me that the cravings of the belly were the greatest consolation to human grief.

I was searching for the snow leopard. But what was I truly searching for? The greatness of lying in wait: you are tracking an animal, but it is your mother who pays a visit.

The landscape was a folding fan. Ribs of rough slopes interspersed with crumpled panels of snow. Drifts of snow collected in corners; the gods cloaked themselves. Munier put it somewhat less affectedly:

"Snow works like a Magnum photographer: in black and white."

The slopes were fleeced by a dozen bharals. They were scudding toward the western escarpments, triggering rockslides. Their panic disturbed the order of things. Were they fleeing the snow leopard? The noises in the camp grew louder: hammering, the roaring of generators, barking. The valley was chafed by the sound of lowing. The children ran after the yaks and herded them back toward the pens, rolling them like hoops toward the valley floor. With twigs and sticks, these kids who were about three feet tall were guiding the stampede. A sudden twist of a yak's head would disembowel them, but the huge herbivores were happy to be led by these small bipeds. The masses had submitted. This was what had happened in the Fertile Crescent 15,000 years before the birth of the crucified anarchist. Men rounded up huge herds. The bovines traded their freedom for security. Their genes remember this pact. This renunciation led beasts to the paddocks and men to the cities. I was of this human-bovine race: I lived in an apartment. Authority dictated my actions and my gestures, and regulated my individual freedoms. In exchange, I was provided with sewage systems and central heating—with fodder, in other words. Tonight, the animals would graze in peace, by which I mean in prison. Meanwhile, the wolves would roam the darkness, the leopards would prowl, the blue sheep would tremble, perched on the rockface. What to choose? A meager life beneath the Milky Way, or food and warmth in the muggy heat of one's own kind?

. . .

WE WERE 300 METERS above the huts. The cliffs tumbled down the slopes toward the Mekong. The yaks were tiny specks on the steppe. The smoke from the stove turned the air blue. The temperature was still falling, nothing was moving, the universe was sleeping. We were snaking between the rocky ledges toward the camp when we heard a growl. This was not a madrigal, it was a howl. A dozen times it echoed around the valley, vast and sorrowful. The snow leopards were calling to each other to perpetuate the stippled species. Where had the cry come from? From the banks of the river or the walls of a cave? A mournful mewling filled the valley. It required great imagination to hear it as a love song. The snow leopards growled and left. "I love him; I flee him," confides Racine's Bérénice, queen of the leopards. Already, I was constructing a theory of love proportionate to the distance maintained between two creatures. The infrequent rhythm of courtship would guarantee the perpetuation of feeling.

"It's the opposite," Munier corrected me as I expounded my barroom philosophy. "They call so that they can find each other. They are choosing each other, searching for each other. The growls are in harmony."

Children of the Valley

Every evening, when we arrived back at the huts, Gompa's sisters would take us by the hand and lead us to the stove. Over the years, they would learn to replicate their mother's gestures which they, in turn, would pass on to their own daughters. We helped them carry water in the Asian manner: two buckets hung at either end of a bamboo pole. It was a heavy load for my battered back. Jisso, who could not weigh more than thirty kilos, never begrudged the 200-meter trek between the river and the camp. Gompa mimicked my efforts, grimacing and hobbling, bent double. Later we dozed in the warmth of the hut. The Buddha smiled. The candles gave off a white smell. The mother poured the tea. The father, wrapped in furs, woke from his nap. The stove was the pole star. Around it, the family constellations: order, balance, security. From outside came the sound of mastication. The slave-animals were resting.

THE SNOW LEOPARD NEVER reappeared. We covered every centimeter of the slopes, explored hollows and caves, encountered foxes, hares and countless herds of blue sheep, but no snow leopard. Meanwhile, the lammergeyers traced circles of death over my disappointment.

I had to resign myself: here, evolution did not depend on multitudes to perpetuate itself. In tropical ecosystems, life breeds in profusion: clouds of mosquitoes, swarms of arthropods, explosions of birds. Life is short, swift, interchangeable: spermatic dynamite. Nature's prodigality replenishes what it loses through the waste of frenzied feeding. In Tibet, the paucity of animals is counterbalanced by their longevity. Here, animals are resilient, individuated, programmed for the long term, the hard life. Herbivores crop the meager grasses. Vultures scythe the empty air. Predators slink home unrewarded. Later they will relaunch their attacks further off, scattering other herds. At times, hours can pass without the slightest movement, the faintest breath.

The wind stripped scabs of snow from the slopes. We were holding firm. The principle of lying in wait is to suffer discomfort in the hope that an encounter will justify this suffering. The idea that the animal was there, that we had seen it, that it could perhaps see us, that it might appear was reason enough to suffer the wait. I remembered how, in Proust's *Recherche*, Swann, besotted with Odette de Crécy, drew satisfaction from the simple knowledge that she might be close at hand, even if he did not encounter her. I vaguely remembered a passage, but I had to wait until I returned to Paris to find it and read it to Munier. Marcel Proust would have perfectly understood the principle of our watchful wait, but in a mink dress-coat, at −20°C, he would have caught cold and coughed. One had only to replace the name Odette with "the snow leopard": "Even before he saw Odette, even if he did not succeed in seeing her there, what a joy it would be to set foot on that soil where, not knowing the exact spot in which, at any moment, she was to be found, he would feel all around him the thrilling possibility of her suddenly appearing . . ." The possibility of the snow leopard thrilled through the mountains. All we asked of it was that it sustain this apprehensive hope that made everything bearable.

That day, the three children came to find me, led by Gompa, the smallest and the most diabolical. They headed straight for me, singing and gamboling, their jackets undone, their hair tousled by the wind. They walked directly to the rocks where I was lying, ruining my attempts to hide and proving that my camouflage was far from perfect. From the valley floor, they had spotted my hide from 500 meters away. They crawled in beside me, lively and endearing, knowing nothing of the world beyond this valley, this life, these tranquil days spent among wild beasts and yaks. At the age of eight, these kids had a sense of freedom, of autonomy, of responsibility, with their snotty noses, their cheeky grins, a stove as second mother and a herd of giants under their command. They feared the snow leopards, but carried small daggers in their belts, and could defend themselves if attacked. Moreover, they warded off their fears with wild shouts into the icy air. They had no guidance counselor; they knew how to navigate the mountains. They spent each day weaving through the promise of narrow gorges that led to cols that opened onto the horizon. They were spared the ignominy of our European childhoods: the *education* that strips children of their gaiety. Their world had its edges; the night, its cold; the summer, its gentle warmth; the winter, its hardships. They lived in a kingdom ringed by towers, pierced by archways, defended by ramparts. They spent no time staring at screens and perhaps their grace was proportionate to the absence of high-speed broadband? Munier, Marie and Léo, hiding at the foot of a cliff on the far bank of the river, came and joined our group. And so, abandoning all hope of surprising the snow leopard, we held court among the rocks until nightfall.

Munier showed the children a print of a photograph he had taken a year earlier.

In the foreground, a falcon the color of leather perched on a lichen-speckled boulder. Behind, slightly to the left, hidden by the curve of the rockface and invisible to the unsuspecting glance, the eyes of a snow leopard staring straight at the photographer. The animal's head merged so completely with the rock that it took a moment for the eye to make it out. Munier had his lens focused on the falcon's plumage, utterly unaware that the leopard was watching him. It was only when studying his prints two months later that he noticed its presence. The infallible naturalist had let himself be duped. When he first showed me the photo, I had seen only the bird and my friend had to point to the leopard before I noticed what my eye would never have detected unprompted, since it sought only to detect an immediate presence. Once seen, I was struck by the presence of the animal every time I saw the photograph. The indistinguishable had become the obvious. The image concealed a valuable lesson. In nature, we are constantly being watched. Our eyes, on the other hand, are drawn to what is simple, they confirm what we already know. A child, being less conditioned than an adult, catches the mysteries of backgrounds and of hidden presences.

Our little Tibetan friends were not taken in. The fingers instantly pointed to the leopard. "*Sa'u!*" they shrieked. Not because their life in the mountains had honed their vision, but because their child's eyes were not drawn to certainty. They explored the peripheries of the real.

Definition of the artist's gaze: seeing big cats hidden behind ordinary screens.

The Second Apparition

We saw it for the second time on a snowy morning. We were perched on the limestone ridges and the southern end of the valley, above a rocky arch lanced by the winds. We had taken up our positions at dawn: the wind lashed at our faces.

Munier remained stoic, his eyes glued to his binoculars. His inner life fed upon the outside world. In him, the possibility of an encounter numbed all pain. The night before, he had talked to me about his family: "They think I'm a neurotic: I'll be watching a nuthatch fly past while important things are going on." I argued, on the contrary, that neurosis lay in the fragmentation of the brain panicked by an overload of information. Being a prisoner of the city, fed by the constant outpouring of new things, I felt diminished as a man. With the funfair in full swing, the washing machine spinning, screens flickering everywhere, I never stopped to ask the question: how is a flight of swans more interesting than Trump's tweets?

To get through the hours spent lying in wait, I would plunge into my memories. I transported myself back to the previous year, to the beaches along the Mozambique Channel, or called up a painting seen in a gallery in Le Havre, or conjured a beloved face. And I would keep those images alive. They were fragile, flying sparks in the rain. The mind floated, staring into the glare. It was not a particularly intense meditation. Eventually, despite the discomfort, time passed. Later, when the sun bathed the world, these visions dissolved.

The blue sheep had staked a claim on the same small valley, perched at the same height on the facing slope. The sun rose over the ridges. In a single movement, all the animals turned toward the light. If the sun were God, it would consider animals more faithful followers than humankind, crowded inside under fluorescent light, indifferent to its glories.

The snow leopard appeared on the ridge. It crept down toward the bharals. Its body flattened against the ground, it padded cautiously—every muscle taut, every movement controlled, a perfect machine. With measured steps, the weapon of mass destruction advanced toward the great dawn sacrifice. Its body flowed between the rocks. The blue sheep did not notice. This is how the snow leopard hunts, using the element of surprise. A heavy animal, incapable of running down a fleeing prey (unlike the cheetah of the African savanna), it relies on camouflage, approaches its prey from upwind, and once within a few meters, pounces. "Lightning attack" is the term used by the military to describe an attack that relies on fury and unpredictability. If it succeeds, an enemy—even one more numerous and more powerful—does not have time to engage its defenses. Surprised, it is defeated.

On this particular morning, the attack failed. A bharal sensed the snow leopard and its convulsions alerted the rest of the flock. To my surprise, the caprids did not run, but turned to face the big cat to let it know that the sneak attack had been exposed. Being vigilant to danger protected the group. A lesson from the blue sheep: the worst enemy is the one that hides.

Snow leopard unmasked, endgame. It crossed the valley as the bharals watched, retreating only a dozen meters to allow it to pass. If the leopard made a sudden movement, the sheep would scatter among the rocks.

The ounce cut a path through the group, scaled the rocks, reached the ridge and once again appeared, framed against the sky, then disappeared down the other side of the ridge. At this point, Léo, who was posted a kilometer to the north, sighted it in his binoculars, as though we had handed over our surveillance operation. To keep us up to date, he whispered short phrases into his radio:

"It's on the ridge . . .

"It's going down the slope . . .

"It's crossing the valley . . .

"It's lying down . . .

"It's up again . . .

"It's climbing the opposite embankment . . ."

And we waited all day long, listening to this poem, in the hope that the leopard would return to our slopes. The animal moved at a leisurely pace; it had its whole life ahead of it. We had our patience. We offered it up.

We saw it again as night was falling over the crenellations of the ridge. It lay down, stretched, got up again, with a rolling gait, it padded away. The big cat's tail whipped the air, then froze, sketching out a question mark: "Will I retain my kingdom against the onward march of your republics?" It disappeared.

"They spend much of the ten years of their existence sleeping," said Munier. "They hunt when the opportunity presents itself, gorge themselves, and live for a week on their reserves."

"And the rest of the time?"

"They sleep. Sometimes twenty hours a day."

"Do they dream?"

"Who knows?"

"When they stare into the distance, are they contemplating the world?"

"I think so," he said.

OFTEN, IN THE ROCKY inlets of Cassis, I would watch squadrons of gulls and wonder: are these animals looking at the landscape? These birds got up in white tie hovered above the setting sun. They were never dirty—immaculate shirtfronts, pearlescent wings. They cleaved the air without beating a wing, surfing the thermals as the horizon smoldered red. They did not hunt. They seemed to be on display, something that belied the idea that they were motivated purely by survival mechanisms. Even a diehard rationalist could not deny the "sense of beauty" in these animals.

The snow leopard alternated between predatory campaigns and languorous siestas. Once sated, it lay on the limestone flags and I suspect it dreamed of the vast plains of steaming meat spread out before it, where it had only to pounce to get its share.

The Measure of Animals

A nd so, during the ten years of its life, the snow leopard embraced a total existence: its body for joy, its dreams for glory. Jacques Chardonne summed up humankind's task in *Le ciel par la fenêtre*: "To live with dignity in uncertainty."

"Motto for a snow leopard!" I said to Munier.

"Careful," he said. "We can persuade ourselves that animals enjoy sunshine, bloody kills and long naps, we can ascribe complex emotions to them—I do it myself—but let's not burden them with morality."

"A human, all too human morality?" I said.

"It's not theirs," he said.

"Vice and virtue?"

"Not their affair."

"Feelings of shame after a massacre?"

"Inconceivable!" said Léo, who had read books.

He reminded us of Aristotle's observation of "in every animal there is a measure of noble life and beauty." With this single phrase in *Parts of Animals*, the philosopher describes all conduct in the wild. Aristotle limited the fate of animals to vital functions and formal perfection, ignoring all moral considerations. The philosopher's intuition was perfect, brilliantly thought, nobly formulated, utterly effective—Greek in other words. Animals occupy their rightful place, without raising their heads above the parapet constructed by the trial and error of evolution, of harmony and equilibrium. Each animal is an element in the engine of order and beauty. The animal is a jewel set into a crown. Were such a diadem to be washed clean of blood. Morality was not party to this organization, nor cruelty to this devourment. Morality was an invention of humankind, which had much to reproach itself for. Life was like a game of pickup sticks, and man was too brutish for such a delicate game. He had burst onto the scene with a violence not always necessary to the survival of his species and, what is more, went beyond the boundaries he had instituted.

"Each animal dispenses its measure of death," Aristotle might have added. Twenty-three centuries later, Nietzsche confirmed this postulate in *Human, All Too Human*: "life has not been devised by morality." No, life has been devised by life itself and its expansionist imperative. The animals in our valley and those across the known world lived beyond good and evil. They were not sating a lust for pride or power.

Their violence was not fury, their hunts were not roundups.

Death was no more than a meal.

The Sacrifice of the Yak

I've spotted a cave about two hundred meters above the road. We'll go and bivouac there, it overlooks the eastern slope, we'll have the best possible position."

With these words Munier woke us, one morning a week after our arrival. It was freezing inside the hut. Léo lit the stove and we first made tea, then packed our kitbags: the former to wake us, the latter to survive the night. We took the cameras, the binoculars and telescopes, sleeping bags to survive in −30°C temperatures, provisions, and my copy of the *Tao Te Ching*.

"We'll stay up there two days and two nights. If it passes, the cave will give us the perfect vantage point."

We ascended via a thalweg, a narrow declivity running at

right angles to the canyon. In the leaden air, it took some time to reach the escarpments. My friends struggled. Léo was carrying thirty-five kilos and the huge telescope stuck out of his pack. So, I thought to myself, even metaphysicians are capable of physical effort. Marie was almost invisible beneath a backpack that dwarfed her. Once again, I carried nothing, I strolled along like a fat man flanked by servants. It was my damaged vertebrae that exempted me from physical exertion, rather than my taste for colonial caravans.

"There's a dark shape over there," said Marie.

The yak was dying. Lying on its left side, it panted, its nostrils spewing plumes of vapor. It would die in this narrow gorge. No more running through the joyous sunlight. The snow leopard's teeth had pierced the neck, blood was spilling onto the snow. The animal was trembling.

This was how leopards hunted, leaping for the withers and not letting go. The animal bolts down the slopes with the leopard clinging to its neck, a flight that ends when predator and prey tumble. They roll together down the bank, over the escarpments and crash onto the rocks. Sometimes, in these struggles, a leopard can break its spine. Those that survive the impact may limp for the rest of their lives. The golden fibulae of Scythian nomads often featured the motif *leopard at the throat*. The carvings depicting a fury of muscle and fur, the dance of fight and flight that is the most common outcome of the meeting of two creatures.

The leopard had heard us. It was probably hiding among the rocks, watching us, worried that these bipeds—a race despised by all—would rob it of its prey. It was mistaken, since Munier's plan was more sophisticated than stealing the animal's food. The yak was dead.

"We're going to drag it ten meters, to the bottom of the gorge, where it can be seen from the cave," said Munier. "If the panther comes back, we'll see it."

By evening, we were in position, the dead yak lay on the grass and we had settled in a system of superposed caves. "A duplex!" Léo said when he discovered the two grottos, one above the other, separated by a thirty-meter rock shelf. Marie and Munier took the lower cave (the Imperial Suite), Léo and I took the upper (the servants' quarters) and the yak lay 100 meters below (the estate cellars).

Fear of the Dark

How many nights had I spent bivouacking in caves? In Provence, in the Alpes-Maritimes, the forests of Île-de-France, in India, in Russia, in Tibet, I had slept in Occitan caves called *balmas* that smelled of figs, on granite overhangs, in volcanic clefts and sandstone nooks. As I entered, I experienced a sacred moment: a sense of gratitude. It was important to disturb nothing. From time to time, I had frightened chiroptera or scolopendra. The ritual was unvarying: level the ground, set down your effects in a corner sheltered from the wind. The cave that Léo and I had just entered had previously been occupied. The ground had been leveled and cleared, the ceiling was black with soot, a circle of stones formed a hearth. Caves had constituted the geographical matrix of humanity during its pitiful begin-nings. Every cave and grotto had provided refuge and shelter until a burst of Neolithic energy urged humans from their shelters. Humankind dispersed, fertilized alluvial plains, do-mesticated herds, invented one God and began the felling of the earth before, 10,000 years later, reaching the acme of civilization: traffic jams and obesity. One might adapt Pas-cal's *pensée* B139—"all the miseries of mankind derive from one single fact, that he cannot stay quietly in a room"—and discover that the miseries of the world began when the first man left the first cave.

In caves, I perceive the magical echo of an ancient radi-ance. My first thought is the same as when I step into the nave of a church: what things have happened here? How did people love beneath this vaulted roof? Is it possible that pri-meval conversations permeated the rock, as vesper psalms imbued Cistercian limestone?

Sometimes, when bivouacking in Provence, my friends would mock these suggestions. They would snigger in their sleeping bags: "You're starting to develop a sexual complex, mate! All this crawling through caves and tunnels is just nos-talgia for the ooze. You're talking psychobabble." They busted my balls with their crude sarcasm.

I loved caves because they harked back to the earliest ar-chitecture, where the twin forces of water and chemical des-iccation succeeded in carving holes in a rockface so that the nights of those passing through might be a little less uncomfortable.

Léo and I placed a sheep's skull on a rock near the cave opening, and this totem to death and power guarded the entrance. Léo set up the cameras. From our position, we could see the yak at the foot of the gorge. So began the wait. A lammergeyer hovered, its wings spread as though to span the two banks of the valley. In the canyon, darkness gathered, cold exacerbated the silence and, as I contemplated the coming hours, I realized what the absence of an inner life would mean at −30°C, even as I cursed my taste for conversation since silence was the order of the day. Léo was remarkable in his role as a statue. He barely moved, surveying the landscape with an almost imperceptible movement of the telescope. I ended up retreating to the back of the cave. Without taking off my mitten, I opened my copy of the *Tao*: "Act without expectation." I thought, "Surely expectation is a form of action?" Surely the expectancy of lying in wait was a form of action since it gave free rein to thought and hope? In which case the Way of the Tao would recommend expecting nothing of expectancy, a thought which made it easier for me to reconcile myself with lying here, in the dust. The Tao has this advantage: its cyclical movement circles in the mind, occupies the time, even in the semi-darkness of a rocky freezer at 4,800 meters. Suddenly, a shadow approached: Léo was coming to the back of the cave.

In the distance, yaks were crossing the slopes. Sometimes one of these huge balls of hair would slip on a patch of névé, and slither down a few meters. Did they know, these hulking guardians, that only an hour earlier, they had just lost one of their own? Did they count, the poor wretches sacrificed to the leopards?

The dark was rising, the snow leopard did not return, we turned on the headlamps fitted with red filters, the sort used by sailors on naval vessels during night watches, to give off as little light as possible. I entertained myself with the thought that I was on the bridge of a galleon of silence launched upon the night where leopards roamed.

The children were rounding up the herd, their voices rose, the darkness now was total. An eagle owl stood guard on the cliff on the far bank of the river. Its hooting announced the opening of the hunting season. "Hoo! Hoo! Sleep, herbivores, and hide yourselves," said the owl, "the raptors are taking wing, the wolves are prowling the darkness, their pupils dilated, and sooner or later the snow leopard will come and bury its muzzle in the belly of one of you."

In the mountains, the sky's efforts in the early hours to hide the traces of night's excesses beneath a layer of snow are not unwelcome.

At eight o'clock, we were joined by Marie and Munier. Léo heated up soup on the timorous flame of a spirit stove. We talked of life in the caves, of fear overcome by fire, of the conversations that sprang from the flames, of dreams that became art, or the wolf that became a dog, and of the courage of humankind to cross the line. Then Munier talked about the human rage that would be unleashed on all other species for the sufferings of those Paleolithic winters. We all returned to our caves.

We crept into the sleeping bags. If the snow leopard came in the night, it would pick up our scent despite the cold. We had to resign ourselves to the depressing thought: "The earth smells of man."[*]

"Léo?" I said before turning off my lamp.

"Yeah?"

"Instead of giving his girlfriend a fur coat, Munier takes her to see the animal wearing it."

---

[*] Ylipe, *Textes sans paroles*. (Ylipe was the pseudonym of the French humorist Philippe Labarthe.)

The Third Apparition

At first light, we crawled out of our sleeping bags. It had snowed and the leopard was standing next to its yak, its jaws daubed in blood, its fur dusted with snow. It had come back before dawn and was now sleeping, its belly full. This was why it was called a snow leopard: it arrived as silently as the snow, and soundlessly crept away, melting into the rocks. It had ripped away the shoulder, the choice of kings. The yak's black coat was marked by a vermillion stain. The leopard had spotted us. Rolling onto its side, it stared up at us and we saw its eyes, cold embers. The eyes said: "We cannot be friends, you are nothing to me, your race is recent, mine is timeless, yours spreads across the earth, disrupting the meter of the poem." This face daubed with scarlet was the soul of the primitive world caught between shadow and dawn. The leopard did not seem apprehensive. Perhaps it had eaten too quickly. It slept for brief periods, head resting on its forepaws, then woke and sniffed the air. A phrase I loved from *Récit secret* by Pierre Drieu La Rochelle was pounding in my brain, and if the animal's proximity had not required complete silence, I would have quoted it to Munier over the radio to explain what I was thinking in that moment: ". . . within me, I knew there was something, something that was not me, something that was much more precious than me." I mentally reformulated the phrase: "Without me there is something, something that is not me, that is not man, something that is precious, a treasure beyond humanity."

It stayed until 10 a.m. Two lammergeyers came to find out what was happening. A huge crow traced a line across the sky: a flat line encephalogram.

I had come for the snow leopard. It was there, dozing less than 100 meters from me. The forest girl whom I once loved when I was someone else—before the fall that left me broken—would have noticed details that I could not perceive, would have explained the thoughts of the snow leopard. For her, I focused all of my energy and attention into my gaze. The intensity we force ourselves to invest in taking pleasure in things is a prayer to those who are absent. They would have liked to be here. It is for them that we are looking at the snow leopard. This animal, this fleeting dream, was the symbol of those we have lost. My mother, dead, the girl, gone away: each apparition brought them back to me.

The snow leopard got to its feet, glided behind the rocks and reappeared on the slope. Its fur blended with the undergrowth, a speckled blur of *poikílos*. This word, from ancient Greek, describes the stippled coat of the animal. The same term describes the sparks of thought. The leopard, like a pagan thought, moving through a labyrinth. Difficult to grasp, pulsing, at one with the world, exultant. Its beauty shimmers in the cold. Stretched between dead things, peaceable and dangerous, ambiguous as the greatest poetry, unpredictable, inconsolable, motley, moiré: this is the *poikílos* leopard.

The spark, the speckle vanished. The snow leopard had volatilized. The radio crackled:

"You got it?" said Munier.

"No, lost it," said Léo.

Accepting the World

So began a day of waiting. In southern Lebanon, in the heart of the district of Sidon, stands a shrine to the Virgin Mary: Our Lady of Awaiting. This was the name I gave to our cave. Léo was the canon. With his telescope, he scanned the mountain until it grew dark. In the lower cave Munier and Marie were probably doing likewise, unless they had found another way to spend the hours. From time to time, Léo dropped onto all fours and crawled to the back of the cave to take a sip of tea, then returned to his vigil. Munier had spoken to us over the radio. He thought the snow leopard had crossed the canyon and was now in the rocky terrace on the far slope: "It's going to rest and keep its eye on its prey—scan the rocks on the facing slope, at the same height."

These hours were our debt to the world. I remained in that pod, perched between the valley and the sky, staring at the mountain. I sat, legs crossed, and gazed at the landscape through my vaporous exhalations. I, who had asked that this journey furnish me with endless surprises, "foolishly fascinated by variety and caprice,"* was content with an icy slope in a shrine. Had I been converted to Wu Wei, the Chinese art of non-doing? There's nothing like thirty degrees below zero to reconcile you to such a philosophy. I did not expect, I did not act. Since the slightest movement allowed an icy blast to seep into our backs, it made me loath to embark on any grand projects. Oh, obviously if a snow leopard had suddenly appeared before my eyes, I would have been thrilled, but nothing was stirring and, in this state of waking hibernation, I did not even feel. Watching from a hide was a truly Asian activity. The Tao imbued this waiting for the unique. There was also something of the teachings of the Bhagavad Gita in the negation of desire. The animal's apparition would change nothing about my mood. "Be not moved in success or failure," as Krishna says in Chapter II.

And as the wide expanse of time molded thought, it occurred to me that this art of waiting into which Munier had

* Gérard de Nerval, *Aurélia*.

initiated me was an antidote to the frenzy of my era. In 2019, pre-cyborg humanity no longer accepted the real, was not satisfied by it, was not in harmony with it, and did not know how to make its peace with it. Here, at Our Lady of Awaiting, I asked nothing of the world but that it continue to furnish what was already there.

In this early twenty-first century, we, the eight billion human beings, subjugated nature with a passion. We razed the ground, acidified the waters, asphyxiated the air. A report by the WWF calculated that population sizes of wildlife had decreased by sixty percent globally over the past five decades. The world was regressing, life was retreating, the gods were in hiding. The human race was in fine fettle. It was building its own hell, was preparing to break the ten billion barrier. Optimists thrilled at the possibilities of a globe inhabited by fourteen billion people. If life amounted merely to satisfying biological needs such that the species could continue to reproduce, the prospects were encouraging: we could copulate in Wi-Fi-enabled concrete cubes and feed on insects. But if we demanded that some measure of beauty be part of our time on earth, and if life was a game played in a magical garden, then the extinction of animals was horrifying news. The worst possible news. The report was greeted with indifference. The railwayman defends the railwayman. Humankind concerns itself with humankind. Humanism is a union like any other.

This disintegration of the world was accompanied by feverish hope in a better future. The more reality deteriorated, the more resounding the messianic imprecations. There is a proportional link between the destruction of the living and the two-pronged movement of forgetting the past and imploring the future.

"Tomorrow, better than today," the grotesque slogan of modernity. Politicians promised reforms ("change," they yelped), believers waited for eternal life, the lab rats of Silicon Valley offered us Humankind 2.0. In a nutshell, we had only to wait, the future would be brighter and better. It was the same old song: "Since the world is in ruins, let's sort out our exit strategy!" Scientists, politicians and ministers all pressed their noses against the shop window of hope. But when it came to preserving what we had inherited, there were few takers.

Here a tribune of the barricades called for Revolution and his troops poured into the streets brandishing pickaxes; there a prophet invoked the *Great Hereafter*, and his flock prostrated themselves before the promise; elsewhere, a digital Dr. Strangelove engineered post-human mutations and his customers became enthralled to technological talismans. People lived from hand to mouth. Unable to bear their circumstances, they waited for the benefits of this parallel world without knowing what it would be like. It is harder to prize what one already has than to dream of impossible worlds.

All three instances—revolutionary faith, messianic hope, technological charity—used the idea of salvation to mask complete indifference to the present. Worse, they spared us the need to behave nobly in the here and now, and saved us from having to treat what was still standing with care.

Meanwhile, ice sheets melted, plastics proliferated, animals died.

"Concocting stories about a world 'other' than this one is utterly senseless."[*] I had noted this proposition by Nietzsche on the blank page of a notebook. I could have carved it above the entrance to our cave. A motto for the valleys.

There were many of us, in the caves and in the cities, who longed, not for an augmented world, but for a world celebrated in fairness and equality, home only to its splendors. A mountain, a sky streaked with shifting light, careening clouds, a yak standing on a ridge: everything was arrayed, ample. What was unseen might appear at any moment. What did not appear had learned to hide.

This was the pagan acceptance of the world.

"Léo, I'm going to recite the Creed," I said.

"I'm listening," he said politely.

"Worship that which is before your eyes. Expect nothing. Remember much. Guard against hopes, those wisps of smoke above the ruins. Exult in what reveals itself. Seek out symbols

---

[*] Nietzsche, *Twilight of the Idols.*

and hold poetry more powerful than faith. Accept the world. Fight so that it survives."

Léo was still scanning the mountain with his telescope. He had been too busy concentrating to really listen, which allowed me to continue my peroration.

"Those who champion home call our acceptance 'resignation.' They are wrong. It is love."

The Last Apparition

It was a showdown between our admiration and the snow leopard's indifference. Munier had been right. The animal had settled on the far slope, 300 meters east, at the same height as we were. Toward 10 a.m. it appeared in the viewfinder. Dozing on a rock ledge, it raised its head and glanced down at the dead yak. Was it making sure that the vultures had not flocked to the spoils? The animal lifted its head toward the heavens, then once more buried it between its paws. It catnapped all day. Given the distance between us, we could talk in normal voices, smoke cigars, and fire up the stoves again, because it felt good to blow on hot soup in that cavernous ice-box. Every couple of minutes I would crawl over to the tripod and press my face to the eyepiece to gaze at its tapering head, its body curled up to preserve the heat. Each time, the sight produced an electric shock of pleasure. Such are the realities whose presence is confirmed by the human gaze. That morning, the snow leopard was not a myth, nor a hope, nor the object of Pascal's wager. It was there. Its reality confirmed its supremacy.

It did not return to its prey. The day seeped away. The funeral service planned by a patrol of carrion feeders (vultures, lammergeyers, corvids) did not take place. From time to time, Munier's voice came over the radio. "A goosander to the west, red-billed chough above the stone arch." Wherever his gaze lingered, he saw animals, or sensed their presence. And this gift, comparable to the wisdom of an erudite *flâneur* who points out a classic column, a Baroque pediment, a neo-Gothic addition, meant that Munier could move through a landscape that was endlessly illuminated and noble, teeming with creatures whose very existence was invisible to the layman's eye. I could understand why my friend lived in isolation in the Vosges. How could he seek the company of peers, this man who had seen big cats come down like the wolf on the fold, and knew why crows soared? He could still be moved by books: "When I left school at seventeen," he told me, "it was so that I could go into the forest. I never opened a textbook again, but I've read everything ever written by Jean Giono."

The snow leopard departed with the night. It got to its

feet, slunk behind a rock and disappeared. We bivouacked in the caves for a second night, hoping it might come back. In the morning, it was nowhere near the carcass. The cold would preserve the yak for some time yet, until beaks and jaws and fangs tore it to shreds. Then its flesh would be reabsorbed into the flesh of other creatures to satiate other hunters. To die is to pass through.

The Eternal Return
of the Eternal Return

We packed away the bivouac and we headed back, Munier, Léo, Marie and I, to the Tibetan hearth; we did not say a word since the snow leopard occupied our thoughts and one does not spoil a dream with small talk.

I have long believed that landscapes determine belief. Deserts conjure an unforgiving God, the Greek islands teem with many gods, cities foster only self-love, while jungles are alive with spirits. The fact that the White Fathers managed to preserve their faith in one God in the midst of forests filled with shrieking parrots seemed to me to be a feat.

In Tibet, the glacial valleys quelled all desire and inspired the idea of a great cycle. Higher still, the plains worn down by storms and tempests confirmed that the world was a wave and life a transition. My soul was ever weak and easily influenced. Dropped into a Yazidi village, I would worship the sun. Washed up on the shores of the Ganges, I would be one with Krishna ("Consider with an equal eye suffering and pleasure"). Sojourning in the Monts d'Arrée in Brittany, I would dream of the Celtic spirits they call Ankou. Only Islam had not taken root, I had no taste for penal law.

Here, in the rarefied air, souls migrated between transient bodies in order to continue their course. Since my arrival in Tibet, I had been thinking about the weight of the recurring lives of animals. If the snow leopard in the valley were an incorporated soul, where would it find refuge after nine years of slaughter? What other beast would be prepared to accept such a burden? How would it break free of the cycle?

To look into the eyes of the snow leopard was to be imbued with the spirit of pre-Adamite times. These same eyes had looked upon early humans when we hunted in small groups, uncertain of survival. What imprisoned soul was beneath that fur? When the ounce first appeared to me, some days earlier, I thought I recognized the face of my late mother: high cheekbones slashed by a harsh gaze. My mother practiced the arts of disappearance, had a penchant for silence, a stiffness that passed for autocratic. To me, that day, the snow leopard was my poor mother. And the idea of the transmigration of souls through the vast planetary stock of living flesh, that same idea formulated in the sixth century before Christ, in places that were geographically remote—Greece and the Indo-Nepalese plain—by Pythagoras and the Buddha, seemed like an elixir of consolation.

We arrived back at the huts. We drank tea before the still faces of the children, licked by the glow of the flames. Silence, shadows, smoke: Tibet was hibernating.

The Forked Source

We had spent ten days in the canyon of the snow leopards. Now Munier wanted to leave to photograph the source of the Mekong. We drove all day to a yak breeders' camp at the foot of a bluff. The plateau was a curved section of steppe blasted by sunlight. To the north, white peaks soared. A few of the yak owners were wintering in an overheated building of corrugated iron, an islet in the midst of the void. A hundred head of yak were grazing on the meager grass bleached yellow by winter. The following morning, at 4 a.m., we left the comfort of the stove and walked along a ribbon of water that our maps insisted was the Mekong. "Carry on uphill for four hours. When you get to 5,100 meters, you'll come to a corrie and the source of the river," we were told by Tsetrin, the guard. So, this was the River of Nine Dragons: a frozen stream. The ice cracked. We walked on the brittle surface, like wary convalescents taking the waters in a frozen canal in Baden-Baden. We encountered the carcass of a yak being picked clean by vultures. The birds ripped at hunks of flesh, took off, flapping wildly as they jostled for space. Until this point, I had been dazzled by the spectacle of death being devoured and reintegrated into life. But the blood-besmirched throats and the fury of feathers rather lessened my desire to one day have my body thrown to the vultures. Once you've seen birds crazed with blood lust, a little plot of chrysanthemums in Yvelines cemetery suddenly seems charming.

We trekked slowly, and I forced myself to believe this was the Mekong, the river of Khmer tears, of gilded colonial nostalgia, of *The 317th Platoon* and the living Buddha, of graceful apsaras and lotus flowers. A rivulet the color of moonlight, virgin, unpolluted.

At 5,100 meters, we found the stele inscribed with Chinese ideograms that probably designated the river's source. Spanning more than 5,000 kilometers, the Mekong flowed through Tibet, China and Indochina to the delta where Marguerite Duras once had a lover. From private ventures to public projects, the waters of the Mekong would bathe works and days. There would be battles. The source of a great river veils the issue of the Orient: why must every source branch out? Why must it fork?

For the moment, a sheet of ice bound a layer of gravel. This was the source, the path, the Tao of the Mekong, ground zero, the fount of the *roman-fleuve*. The flow would converge, cutting a path through the mountain. The balmy air would liberate the waters, the trickle would proliferate with life: first microorganisms, and later fish of increasing voracity. The river would swell. A fisherman would cast his net onto the waters, villagers would quench their thirst from it, a factory would dump waste into it: when humankind is involved, everything ends up in a sewer. As the altitude declined, wild barleys would grow. Lower down, tea, wheat and finally rice, and one day fruits would appear on boughs. Water buffalo would wallow. From time to time, a leopard in the reeds would snatch a child. People would quickly find consolation; there are so many born. At still lower altitudes, women would daily come to draw water already teeming with bacteria, canals would be dug to provide irrigation. Skin tones would darken. Girls would dry orange sheets on stone jetties and teenage boys would dive from rocky outcrops, then the current would slow, the meanders widen in their own alluvial deposits, the river would raise its banks and the horizon would unfold, an irrigated plain illuminated by hydroelectric plants upstream. On market days, barges would float bow to bow, snakes would swim between half-charred bodies, while countries disputed the riverbanks as they became borders. Patrols would intercept smugglers. Business would carry on and eventually the waters would merge with the sea. Pallid tourists would splash in the waves. Would they even know that snow leopards had drunk from these waters, back when they belonged to the heavens?

Here, destiny was born. The animals Munier tracked were also born of a single source. They too had branched and forked. The snow leopard evolved from a branch some five million years ago. If life on earth were compared to a river, it too had its source, its bed, its backwaters. Its course was unfinished; its delta unknown. We human beings had emerged from a very recent fork. In the plates of my childhood biology books, the evolutionary branching was represented by graphics that resembled river estuaries. Every source is oblivious to its capabilities.

We stayed in the gravel corrie for an hour, then headed down, slipping and sliding all the way. Munier was looking for an animal. To him, an empty landscape was a tomb. Thankfully, at 4,800 meters, a wolf was rolling in a patch of névé. Munier was happy.

Back at the camp, we mentioned our encounter with the wolf; the herdsman talked to us about their annual visits: one or two snow leopards in winter, wolves almost every day. But as he talked, he stoked the stove so much that we dozed off. Sleep swept away the vision of the source.

In the Primordial Soup

We headed back toward Yushu by hill and dale, never varying from an altitude of 4,000 meters. By nightfall, we were on a road that led to some thermal springs hidden in the cliff face. Two wolves darted through the headlights. The beams picked out their saffron coats—a flash in the night. Munier jumped down from the jeep. The sight of these two jailbirds loping through the darkness, heading for some smash and grab, excited my friend. He sniffed the icy air deeply, trying to detect the spoor. He had seen hundreds of wolves, in Abyssinia, in Europe, in America. He was never satisfied.

"You don't get out of the car when a man passes," I said.

"The man will pass again. Wolves are rare."

"Man is a wolf to man," I said.

"If only."

We had reached the thermal springs. At 10 p.m. we pitched camp in the shelter of a slope, it was −25°C, then Marie, Munier and I splashed in the scalding water, invisible in the clouds of steam. Up above, whipped by the wind, Léo watched over the camp. The water gushed beneath an indent in the rock. We had had to slide along the overhang. Munier was familiar with the place, having played the Japanese macaque here the previous year. He described the snow monkeys that frequented the hot springs of Nagano, steam blurring their red faces, wet tufts of hair turning to stalactites.

But, that night, we looked more like Russian apparatchiks in a sauna divvying up the resources of the region. We lit some fine Cuban cigars (Epicure No. 2) that we had kept safe in aluminum tubes. Our skin took on the texture of a toad's belly and our Havanas the texture of marshmallow. The stars shimmered.

"We're splashing in the primordial soup," I said. "We're bacteria at the dawn of the world."

"We're a little better off," said Marie.

"Bacteria should never have crawled out of the cauldron," said Munier.

"But then we'd never have had Beethoven's Triple Concerto," I said.

The fossils embedded in the vault did not date from the beginnings of the world. They were merely a recent episode in the adventure. Life had been born of the globe of water, matter and gas that formed 4.5 billion years ago. Biotics proliferated in every nook and cranny without any apparent semblance (beyond the will to propagate), thereby creating lichen, rorquals and us.

The whorls of cigar smoke caressed the fossils. I knew their names, having collected them between the ages of eight and twelve. I said them aloud, since scientific taxonomy serves as a poem: ammonites, crinoids, trilobites. Some of these creatures were more than 500 million years old. They had reigned. They had had their concerns: defending themselves, feeding, perpetuating the species. They were mostly small and distant. They had disappeared and we human beings who ruled the earth (from a recent date, for an undetermined period) paid them scant attention. And yet their lives had been a stage on the road to our appearance. Suddenly, living creatures dragged themselves from the bath. A few—the more adventurous—had crawled onto a shore. They took in a mouthful of air. And it was to this breath that we, humans and other animals of the open air, owed our existence.

Getting out of this bath was not one of the more pleasant moments of my existence. I had to walk naked across warm algae, jump into my Chinese boots, pull on the huge fur-lined jacket and make it back to the tent in temperatures of −20°C.

That is: drag myself from the soup, crawl through the darkness, find shelter: the story of life in a nutshell.

Homeward, Perhaps . . .

The following day, we drove on across the plateau toward Yushu. The driver hurtled down the road muttering prayers that made mention of lotuses. He seemed in a hurry to get home, or maybe to die. Lulled by the humming sound, by unconscious imitation, I found myself humming Heraclitus' *Panta Rhei*: "everything flows, everything passes, everything fades," which I transformed into a psalm of my own: "Everything dies, everything is reborn, everything returns that it may perish, everything feeds on itself." We were coming closer to the city. Already, we could see ragged beggars crawling toward the temple. They thought as Heraclitus did, but they did not rejoice in this general flux.

They attempted to acquire merits so that they would not be reborn as dogs, or worse, as tourists. They longed to escape the eternal rebirth. This endless cycle was their curse. The driver carefully slowed as we passed the temple, he did not want to run over a pilgrim and thereby aggravate his flaws. I stared at the pilgrims through the window. Our technological world had become animal, that is to say mobile. In the West, prevailing thought in the early twenty-first century considered as virtues the movement of people, the circulation of goods, the fluctuation of capital, the fluidity of ideas. "Clear off!" commanded the authorities of the planetary roundabout. Until this point, civilizations had developed according to the vegetal principle. This consisted of putting roots down through the centuries, extracting the nutrients of the land, building pillars and favoring expansion beneath the unchanging sun by protecting itself from the neighboring plant with thorns and spines. Things had changed: now it was important to move fast, to move ceaselessly through the global savanna. "Get marching, men of earth. Move along! There's nothing much left to see here!"

At the last mountain pass before Yushu, the brakes failed. Using the handbrake, the driver negotiated the bends and increased the frequency of his mantras. By a strange and morbid Buddhist reflex, as soon as he realized that the brakes had failed, he pumped the accelerator. And under the auspicious influence of my fatalism, I found myself thinking that this was logical. What did ending it all matter in this perfect morning? The mountains glittered, on the rocky ledges animals reigned, and our accident would in no way affect the movement of the last snow leopards.

The Consolation of the Wild

If I hadn't encountered a snow leopard, would I have been bitterly disappointed? Three weeks in the ozone had now been enough to kill the European rationalist in me. I still preferred dreams that came true to the indolence of hope.

In case of failure, the Eastern philosophies brewed on the plains of Tibet or the blaze of the Ganges would have provided me with consolation in the form of renunciation. If the snow leopard had not appeared, I would have taken pleasure in its absence. This was the fatalistic approach of Peter Matthiessen: seeing in his failure the vanity of all things. This is also the approach of La Fontaine's fox: he scorns the grapes once he knows he cannot have them.

I could have trusted to the wisdom of the Bhagavad Gita. I could have followed Krishna's injunction to Arjuna: be not moved in success or failure. "The snow leopard is before you, rejoice, and if it be not there, likewise rejoice," he would have whispered to me. Oh, what opium is the Bhagavad Gita, and how right Krishna was to make the world a flat plain relief battered by the winds of equanimity, another word for sleep!

Or perhaps I would have turned to the Tao. I would have considered absence equivalent to presence. Not seeing the snow leopard would have been a way of seeing.

As a last resort, there was the Buddha. The Prince of the gardens revealed that nothing is more painful than anticipation. I would simply have to slough off the desire to encounter an animal leaping among the rocks.

Asia, an inexhaustible moral pharmacopeia. The West, too, had its remedies. One Christian, the other more recently minted. Catholics heal their sufferings by a semi-narcissistic, semi-Christlike approach that consists of rejoicing in one's disappointment: "Lord, if I did not have a vision of the snow leopard, it is because I was not worthy to receive it, and I am grateful to You for sparing me the vanity of such an encounter." Modern man had also devised a viaticum: recrimination. One had only to cast oneself as a victim to avoid admitting failure. I could have lamented: "Munier set the hides in the wrong place, Marie made too much noise, my parents left me shortsighted! And as if that wasn't enough, rich people shot the snow leopards, poor me!" Finding someone to blame took up time and precluded introspection.

But I needed no consolation because I had glimpsed the handsome face of the spirit of the stones. The image, slipping beneath my eyelids, lived on in me. When I closed my eyes, I could see the haughty feline face, the folds of fur around the terrible yet delicate maw. I had seen the snow leopard, I had stolen fire. I carried the spark within me.

I HAD LEARNED THAT patience was a supreme virtue, the most elegant, the most neglected. It made it easier to love the world rather than claiming to transform it. It urged one to sit before the scene, to exult in the spectacle, be it only the quivering of a leaf. Patience was humankind's reverence for what was bestowed.

What quality made it possible to paint a picture, to write a sonata or a poem? Patience. It always brought its rewards, its delicate fluctuations offering both the risk that time will seem long and a method for never becoming bored.

To wait was to pray. Something was coming. And if nothing came, it was because we had not known how to look.

The Hidden Face

The world was a jewel box. The jewels were increasingly rare, since humankind had helped itself to much of the treasure. Sometimes, you might see a diamond in front of you. In such moments, the earth glittered and glinted. The heart beat faster, the mind was enriched by the vision.

Wild animals were fascinating because they were invisible. I had no illusions: it was impossible to penetrate their mystery. They belonged to a past from which biology had distanced us. Humanity had declared total war on them. The extermination was almost complete. We had nothing to say to them; they had withdrawn. We had triumphed, and soon we humans would be alone, wondering how we managed to clear everything out so quickly.

Munier had offered to lift a corner of the veil for me, so that I could watch the wanderings of the princes of the earth. The last snow leopards, chirus and kiangs survived, constantly tracked, forced into hiding. To see one was to see a glorious vanished order: an ancient pact between animals and men—the former going about the business of surviving, the latter writing poems and inventing gods. For some inexplicable reason, Munier and I felt nostalgic for this ancient allegiance. "Somber faith in fallen things."*

The earth had been a sublime museum.

Unfortunately, humankind was no curator.

To WAIT AND WATCH requires keeping the soul in suspense. The practice taught me a secret: it is always best to fine-tune one's own reception frequency. Never have I experienced such a keen quivering of the senses as I did during those weeks in Tibet. Once home, I would continue to try to look at the world with all my strength, to scrutinize the shadows. What matter if there was no snow leopard on the itinerary. Waiting and watching is a way of life. In doing so, life does

---

* Victor Hugo, *Les Châtiments*.

not pass by unnoticed. It is something that can be done under a lime tree outside your house, while staring at clouds in the sky, or sitting at a table with friends. More things happen in this world than we think.

The airplane, that great vehicle. The morning flight took us to Chengdu. Léo was reading. Marie stared at Munier who gazed out the window. Love, then, did not mean "looking in the same direction." Marie was thinking of the future, Munier was saying farewell to the snow leopards. I was thinking of the women I loved who were absent. Each leopard that had appeared had offered me a fragment of them.

Chengdu, population fifteen million, unknown to Europeans. To the Chinese, a middle-sized market town. To us, a spermatic matrix straight out of the nightmares of Philip K. Dick, with neon lighting every street and sides of meat in shop windows reflected in the puddles.

At midnight, we were strolling through the placid, uniform crowd that moved in slow waves. A strange vision for me, a French petit-bourgeois: a homogeneous civilian crowd with no military training, without being ordered to do so, marching in step.

The following day, we would fly back to Paris. Right now, we had a night to kill. We headed toward the park in the center of the city. Munier shouted: "Up there!"

A screech owl was fluttering toward the park, wings flickering in the laser beams. Even here, Munier was attuned to the wild. A man's complicity with the animal world makes whole days spent in urban cemeteries bearable. I told Marie and Léo the story of the Polynesian fisherman Tava'e, who spent months cast adrift on the Pacific in a dinghy, and every day contemplated the plankton he collected in a bucket, even going so far as to talk to the micro-organisms. Doing so spared him from coming face-to-face with himself, with despair.

To look at an animal is to press one's eye to a magical spyhole. On the other side of the door, other worlds. No words to describe them, no brush to paint them. At best, one might capture a glimmering. William Blake, in *The Marriage of Heaven and Hell*: "How do you know but ev'ry Bird that cuts the airy way, / Is an immense world of delight, clos'd by your senses five?" Yes, William! Munier and I understood that we did not understand. That was enough to make us happy.

Sometimes, it was not even necessary to see an animal. The mere evocation of their existence was a balm. As Romain Gary describes in *The Roots of Heaven*, prisoners in Nazi death camps kept their spirits up by describing elephant stampedes on the African savanna.

We reached the park. The funfair was a complete success. The rides were whirling, the speakers throbbing, the steam from hot doughnuts shrouded the flickering lights. Even Pinocchio would have been disgusted. The posters did not fail to rehash party propaganda. The Chinese people had lost on both the swings and the roundabouts. Politically, they were subject to socialist coercion. Economically, they were spinning in the capitalist washing machine. They were the fall-guys in this modern farce that flew the flag emblazoned with the hammer and algorithm.

What place was there for a screech owl in a world of lasers? How would snow leopards survive the global hatred of solitude and silence, the last comforts of the miserable?

But, in the end, why worry? There were still thrilling roller coasters and ice creams. Why complain? The funfair was in full swing, why not join in, who cares about animals when you've got carousels and candy floss?

Munier begged us to leave the park. The funfair was getting on his nerves—and he had nerves of steel. As he walked out the gate, he pointed to the sky: "Look at the moon!" It was a full moon. "That's the last untamed world visible to the naked eye. In the funfair, we couldn't see it for the strings of fairy lights."

He did not know that, the following year, the Chinese would land a robot on the dark side of the moon.

We were done with the earth.

It was time that the universe learned what humankind was capable of.

Darkness was prevailing.

Farewell, snow leopards.

AUTHOR'S NOTE

The photographs of Tibetan fauna taken by Vincent Munier during his many trips to the high plateau are published in the book *Tibet minéral animal*, published by Kobalaan (with poems by Sylvain Tesson).

Glossary

apsaras: water sprites

bharal: Himalayan blue sheep (*Pseudois nayaur*)

balmas baume **(Old French),** *balma* **(Occitan):** cave

Beauceron: sheepdog from central France, aka *bas rouge* (red stockings)

corrie: an armchair-shaped hollow found on the side of a mountain

detrital cone: debris deposited in a conical shape, usually carried down by small streams or snow avalanches

firn: crystalline or granular snow

Gévaudan: historical area of southern France in the département of Lozère

glacis: a sloping bank in front of a fort that exposes attackers to the defenders' missiles

karst: an area that has been eroded into fissures and towers

loess: fine, mineral-rich dust carried on the wind that is unusually fertile

névé: between snow and ice, young snow that has been partially melted then refrozen

pediplain: plain formed in a desert where the slopes of multiple peaks meet

piedmont: landform created at the foot of a mountain or mountains by debris brought down by streams

plantigrade: walking with the entire sole of the foot touching the ground

poikílos **(ancient Greek):** spotted, embroidered, in modern usage variegated

scoria: rock formed by lava ejected as fragments from a volcano

scree: small loose stones that form or cover a mountain slope

sisu: Finnish concept described as stoic determination, grit, bravery, resilience

taiga: swampy coniferous forest of high northern steppes

White Fathers, *Pères Blancs:* members of the Society of the Missionaries of Africa

NOTES

Translation excerpts come from the following sources:

33   **"To make the object appear . . ."**: Jean Baudrillard, Preface to *Charles Matton—Palais de Tokyo, 1987* (Paris: Conseil Assouline et Communication Graphique, 1987).

45   **Novalis: *Pollen (Blüthenstaub)*:** *Pollen and fragments: Selected poetry and prose of Novalis* translated by Arthur Versluis (Grand Rapids, Mich.: Phanes Press, 1989).

56   **"Carrying body and soul and embracing the one, can you avoid separation?":** Lao Tzu, *Tao Te Ching*, translated by Gia-fu Feng and Jane English (New York: Vintage, 2012), Chapter 10.

57   *Nameless: the origin of heaven and earth . . .*: Lao Tzu, *Tao Te Ching*, translated by Stephen Addiss and Stanley Lombardo (Indianapolis: Hackett Publishing, 1993), Chapter 10.

68   *The ten thousand things stir about . . .*: Ibid., Chapter 16.

69   *"All things originate from . . ."*: Ibid., Chapter 40.

73   **"man dwells poetically on this earth"**: Hölderlin, "In Lovely Blue" from *Hymns and Fragments*, translated by Richard Sieburth (Princeton: Princeton University Press, 1984).

100   **"the sexual passions of these animals are very violent"**: *The Natural History of Pliny*, Book VIII, translated by John Bostock (London: Henry G. Bohn, 1857).

103   **Peter Matthiessen, *The Snow Leopard***: Peter Matthiessen, *The Snow Leopard* (London: Viking Press, 1978).

105   **"that which emerges and, as emerging, abides"**: Martin Heidegger, quoted in J. J. Kockelmans, *Heidegger on Art and Art Works* (Berlin: Springer, 1985), p. 205.

123   **"Even before he saw Odette . . ."**: Marcel Proust, *Swann's Way*, translated by C. K. Scott Moncrieff (London: Chatto & Windus, 1922), p. 260.

134   **"life has not been devised by morality"**: Friedrich Nietzsche: *Human, All Too Human*, translated by Marion Faber (London: Penguin Classics, 1994).

145   **Ylipe, *Textes sans paroles***: Philippe Ylipe, *Textes sans paroles* (Paris: Le Dilettante, 2001).

152   **Gérard de Nerval, *Aurélia***: Gérard de Nerval, *Aurélia ou le rêve et la vie* (Paris: Revue de Paris, 1855).

152   **"Be not moved in success or failure"**: *Bhagavad Gita*, translated by Simon Brodbeck (London: Penguin Classics, 2003), Chapter II.

NOTES

155 **"Concocting stories about a world . . ."**: Friedrich Nietzsche, *Twilight of the Idols*, translated by Duncan Large (Oxford: Oxford University Press, 2008).

184 **Victor Hugo, *Les Châtiments***: Victor Hugo, *Les Châtiments* (Paris: Henri Samuel et Cie, 1852).

ABOUT THE AUTHOR

Sylvain Tesson has walked from Russia to India, partici-
pated in archaeological expeditions in Afghanistan and
Pakistan, and wintered alone in a cabin on a lake in Siberia.
He earned a diplôme d'études appliquées in geopolitics at the
University of Paris VIII. One of France's most celebrated
writers, he has been awarded the Prix Médicis essai and the
Prix Goncourt de la nouvelle. An international bestseller,
The Art of Patience won the Prix Renaudot in 2019.

A Note on the Type

The text of this book was set in Bembo MT Pro. The display used throughout is Stempel Garamond LT Std.